Circles of Silence

51406

The spiritual life is nothing else but the working of the spirit of God within us, and therefore our own silence must be a great part of our preparation for it, and much speaking . . . will be often no small hindrance of that good which we can only have from hearing what the spirit and voice of God speaks within us. This is not enough known by religious persons . . .

William Law (1686-1761)

No one who ignores the needs of others can hope to walk in the light of contemplation, because their way has turned aside from truth, from compassion and therefore from God.

Thomas Merton (1915-68)

Circles of Silence

EXPLORATIONS IN PRAYER WITH JULIAN MEETINGS

Edited by ROBERT LLEWELYN

DARTON·LONGMAN + TODD

First published in 1994 by
Darton, Longman and Todd Ltd
1 Spencer Court
140-142 Wandsworth High Street
London SW18 4JJ

ISBN 0-232-52091-7

A catalogue record for this book is available
from the British Library

Thanks are due to the Dean and Chapter of Salisbury Cathedral
for permission to reproduce the *Walking Madonna* by Elizabeth Frink.

Phototypeset by Intype, London
Printed and bound in Great Britain
at the University Press, Cambridge

Contents

Preface

The advisory group of Julian Meetings, mindful of their twenty-first anniversary this autumn, have asked me to prepare a book gathering together the best articles and poems from their triannual magazine first published in 1974. Searching through the back numbers has been a rewarding task, and I hope that readers will find themselves equally rewarded in discovering that so much rich material may now be more widely read.

Julian Meetings came into being in 1973 in response to letters written by Hilary Wakeman to a number of Church papers. She had for some years been conscious of a gap in the worshipping life of the Church. At that time many were becoming aware, and particularly the young, that the contemplative dimension of prayer expressed through silence (though not necessarily exclusively so), played little or no part in Christian worship. Hence, as Hilary explains in her introduction (page 4), many began to look elsewhere, and especially to the East, for ways to fill the vacuum.

Whatever gains there may have been, there was undeniably a loss in breaking free from the rich heritage that the Church offers through its historical and doctrinal foundations, its ordered life of worship and its dispensation of Word and sacraments. Moreover, the movement should never have been necessary, for the Church has an immense experience of the contemplative life reaching back to its early days. Witness to this may be found in Professor Owen Chadwick's article about John Cassian on page 34.

Hilary was fortunate in having Michael Ramsey as Archbishop of Canterbury when what she calls her crazy ideas were first revolving in her mind. Although he played no part in the formation of Julian Meetings, Michael Ramsey believed, and it was something of an innovation at the time, that in God's plan the contemplative life was for all Christians. We have to be clear that contemplation is a gift from God and that the most that we can do is to dispose ourselves, through grace, to receive it. But it is our failure, as he would have said, through want of commitment and singleness of purpose, and not God's failure, which may prevent that gift being offered.

In Michael Ramsey's early days as a priest, as I myself can well remember, the contemplative life was generally presented as being open only to the specialist, in this case the monk or nun (and only some at that!). When it came to the ordinary lay person, and even the secular priest, they had generally to be content to limit their personal prayer life to discursive meditation or, in the case of the more advanced, to some simple form of affective prayer; leading perhaps, often through the office, to the threshold of contemplation.

Discursive meditation may be described as a way of prayer in which the mind and imagination play on a passage, usually scriptural, moving on to the making of a resolution arising from the considerations formed. Although this is not to be disparaged, for meditation and contemplation need one another, there comes a time when those moving forward will no longer be able to see discursive meditation as their *real* prayer life. It has been well said that whereas meditation is a turning from the consideration of the things of the world to attend to the things of God, contemplation is a turning from the consideration of the things of God to attend to God himself. And this, of course, is an immensely richer occupation.

At almost the same time as Hilary was writing her invitatory letter to the Church papers, Archbishop Ramsey was writing in the *Canterbury Pilgrim*.

> 'Mystical experience is given to some. But contemplation is for all Christians. Allow me to say a word about that prayer which is indeed for all of us ... (It) means essentially our being with God, putting ourselves in his presence, being hungry and thirsty for him, wanting him, letting heart and mind and will move towards him; with the needs of the world on our heart. It is a rhythmic movement of the personality into the eternity and peace of God, and no less for the turmoil of the world for whose sake as for ours, we are seeking God. If that is the heart of prayer then the contemplative part of it will be large. And a Church which starves itself and its members in the contemplative life deserves whatever spiritual leanness it may experience.'

It is clear how much Julian Meetings owe to Hilary Wakeman, its founder and unfailing guide over these years. Naturally, as the movement has grown the work has become increasingly widely shared. In 1982, Mrs Pamela Fawcett, associated with the enterprise from the first, took over the editorship of *The Julian Meetings Magazine*, then a simple newsletter offering guidance to early groups. Under Pamela's dedicated direction it has grown into a journal devoted to the subject of prayer, understood in its widest sense, and has drawn on many experienced and well-known writers. Equally importantly, and this she would want to stress, it has given the opportunity for non-professionals - amateurs in the true sense, *amator* being the Latin for lover - to make their contribution to a subject which has grown to be the guiding principle of their lives.

My thanks are personally due to Pamela for helping me to trace most of the contributors to this book. Where possible they have been asked for permission to include their writings and given the opportunity of making amendments. Even so, it has not been possible to trace everyone - it is likely that some have died - and I have assumed that none would object to their contributions being printed.

Mrs Hilary Burn is another who has been caught up in the movement from its early days bringing to her work, as an associate writes, 'a combination of quiet efficiency and lightness of touch which is quintessentially Julian Meetings'. She has been guide and mentor to many, has helped to form a number of groups through the sending out of the magazine and general literature, and has been treasurer since 1976.

Since 1990, a part of Hilary's work has been taken over by Mrs Sue Brock who now distributes the magazine and pamphlets. The current subscription for the magazine is £3 a year; readers who would like more details about Julian Meetings literature may write to Sue at 80 Herbert Road, Rainham, Gillingham, ME8 9HP.

There are now nearly 300 groups in the United Kingdom, as well as others in Africa, Australia, and the United States of America. If any in the United Kingdom wish to be put in touch with a group in their neighbourhood they should write to Mrs Gail Ballinger. Gail will also be pleased to offer guidelines to any who would like to set up a group in their area. Her address is The Parsonage, Sambourne Lane, Sambourne, Redditch, Worcs, B96 6PA.

I would like to thank Mrs Jean Dale, well represented in these pages and a long-standing member of the advisory group, for the information and help she has given me.

Throughout its years the editors of *The Julian Meetings Magazine* have received many poems offered for publication. A selection chosen by Miss Dorothy Bartholomew, formerly headmistress of the Norwich High School for Girls, has been included here. Dorothy has for many years been associated with Julian Meetings and I am most grateful for the help which she has graciously given.

Our preface began with the importance of contemplative prayer and it is fitting it should end on the same note. In a recent issue of the *Fairacres Chronicle*, the journal of the Sisters of the Love of God, Mother Anne, superior of the community, drew attention to some words spoken by a retreat leader given many years ago. 'True knowledge is not earthly wisdom, but the result of contemplation looking Godward. Gazing Godward with long, deep attention till at last the light dawns and grows and shines.'

Mother Anne comments: 'There is without doubt plenty of knowledge in our world and a quick readiness to pronounce answers. We know the pain, distress and darkness of so much of our world at the present time, but if, instead of blaming horror videos, the Church's lack of moral teaching or someone else's greed, we could dare to gaze "Godward with long, deep attention", we might all find ourselves looking at the world from a different perspective, with *Kyrie eleison* on our lips and in our hearts'.

Here is the true back to basics and the only one which can save us all.

Robert Llewelyn
Norwich, 1994

Beginnings...

HILARY WAKEMAN

Nobody could have planned such a crazy thing. After a few years we could see that it had all been done by the Holy Spirit. It certainly wasn't what I had in mind when, twenty-one years ago, I wrote a letter to some church papers asking if there were any other people who'd like to form a religious order for ordinary people of all denominations, living in the ordinary world but practising contemplative prayer.

It was 1973. Meditation was big: the very word was for most people synonymous with Eastern religions, and the influence of the Beatles was still strong in spreading Transcendental Meditation. As someone who had come through years of atheism and agnosticism back into Christianity with great joy, and had rediscovered the wordless and imageless prayer of my childhood, I was amazed that the Church was not speaking of its own tradition of meditation.

Of course, there was a problem with words. To most Christians meditation meant a thinking process – the mulling over of a biblical passage for example – while the word in its Eastern sense was closer to what Christians called contemplative prayer. But why was no one talking about it, I wondered? Why were the churches letting so many people say that Christianity didn't have the real spirituality they were looking for and go all the way, metaphorically or physically, to the East for it?

The letter came out of my own needs too. For local rather than theological reasons I'd become a member of the Church of England. A desire for a greater sense of commitment almost led to my becoming a tertiary, a fringe member, of an Anglican women's religious order. Very traditional, and furnished in every sense with polished Victorian gloom. A family crisis at the eleventh hour prevented my formal reception, and within hours I saw that I had in fact been saved. I realised that what I was really seeking was something much broader: I wanted an ecumenical order, based on the practice of contemplative prayer, for ordinary people.

No such order existed, I discovered, I didn't know where to start to make it exist but there seemed a sort of inevitability about the need to try. I knew the Archbishop of Canterbury was Michael Ramsey, so I wrote to him. He replied that he would always encourage those called to live as an order, but that any such group had to make its own plans. But I didn't know any other people who wanted to be that group. I wrote to Archbishop Cardinal Heenan. He said it might be better to become affiliated to something that already existed. I wrote to Metropolitan Anthony of Sourozh. He replied that he understood what I was aiming at but that it had been tried before and had been a flop. So I wrote to the Church papers.

The letter was published by the *Church Times*, the *Catholic Herald*, the *Baptist Times* and *Reform*, the magazine of the United Reformed Church. It began by describing the turning East of so many, and asked:

> Might there not be, on an ecumenical basis, a coming together of Christian lay people interested in, or already practising, contemplative or mystical prayer, with a view to becoming a new type of Order: an association of lay people of all branches of Christianity who wish to dedicate their lives formally to God: married or unmarried, remaining in their own homes and occupations, living lives of simplicity and spiritual discipline, worshipping in their own churches but coming together from time to time; being in some way visually identifiable – by clothing or badge – and showing forth in the world joy and peace and love. . . . Such an Order would bring together those trying to combine contemplative and secular lives, and commend this state to others. It would seek to attract those who would otherwise turn to Eastern religions or cults and it might be a small but useful part of the ecumenical movement. . . . Would anyone interested please get in touch with me?'

The response was wonderful. Within a week or two I had 166 letters. Dividing them geographically, I picked from each area one correspondent who seemed likely to be both enthusiastic and efficient, and wrote asking them to find a room in their city where we could meet on a particular date, and a bed for the night for me. When the plans were made others who had written from that area were informed.

My husband agreed to look after our five young children for a few days, and in the last week of May 1973 I drove across the south of England to Oxford, Exeter and Chichester. Looking back, it was all very naive. If the organiser had been a mature member of the clergy (as I now am) it would have been very different. And the Julian Meetings would probably never have happened.

I had suggested that when we met, it should be for an afternoon and an evening, 'with occasional breaks for silent prayer, or a bite to eat and a cup of tea'. This was to give plenty of time just to talk, to find out why each one had responded and what we all really wanted. What people wanted, it turned out, was very different from what I had proposed in the letter.

Of the twenty who had written from the Oxford area, the ten who met didn't like the word 'Order' and didn't want a Rule of Life. But they were a very ecumenical group, and keen to start meeting regularly. At Exeter the four out of fourteen who met said they wanted an Order, but no Rule of Life – and definitely no advertising. At Chichester six very enthusiastic people met, out of eleven, and were keen to formulate a simple Rule, to produce a booklist and to have an annual national meeting. They arranged to meet monthly in the cathedral.

One week the following month I drove up to Durham, Glasgow, Manchester and Leicester and met with people there. It began to be clear that what nearly everyone wanted was simply to meet regularly with others who practised contemplative prayer. Many had met with incomprehension from their local clergy when they talked about it. Some had even been told that it was 'of the Devil' and should be abandoned at once. Quite a few had thought they must be going mad to pray in this way since no one else they knew seemed to understand it. Their joy at finding others like them was marked, and the possibility of mutual support and encouragement was clearly what brought them together.

In the autumn, meetings were held in Cardiff, Cambridge, Kent and London, and by March 1974 the movement had a magazine – and a name.

We had asked for suggestions for a name, and the word 'Julian' came from every quarter. This was partly because the 600th anniversary of the 'showings' of Julian of Norwich had been celebrated the previous year. But also she seemed the right name for us because as she was pre-Reformation we could in a sense all claim her; and as no one really knows whether she was a lay woman or a professed religious she seemed right for a movement where already it was clear that clergy and lay people all met on an equal footing. So we became 'The Julian Meetings'. It sounded fresh and simple.

It was Canon Keith Walker, then of Chichester Cathedral, who organised our first national meeting. The Cowley Fathers welcomed thirty-three of us to their London house one day in December 1974. Some twenty JM groups were represented. Many talked of the need for the Church to take more seriously the teaching of prayer. An Anglican priest said that he was horrified when he asked a friend why she was about to follow an Eastern guru and she said, 'Because *you* have never taught me to pray'. It was agreed then that the purpose of the Julian Meetings was to foster the practice and teaching of contemplative prayer within the Christian tradition.

We talked about organisation, and agreed that each group should develop in its own way, and that central organisation should be minimal with just a convenor and two advisers. Initially, I was to be the convenor and the advisers would be Keith Walker and Arthur Middleton, an Anglican priest from the north-east of England. It now seems odd that all three of us were Anglicans, a situation that hardly emphasized our ecumenical intentions; but one that would never happen again.

Growing

There is something very precious about the early days of such a movement, when those who find themselves involved become grateful for each other's presence and enthusiastic about being part of this new and unique thing that is happening. Those who came to the second annual meeting took on various tasks: a young Catholic poet and linguist from Cambridge, David Singleton, was to compile a list of the groups: Diana Roantree, then an Anglican from Essex was to find out if the original idea of an Order was still viable, Brian Wills of the Society of Friends and from Hampshire would help me with the thrice yearly newsletter and his wife Pat would duplicate letters and forms. David Smith, an Anglican priest from Lincolnshire, volunteered to compile a list of speakers on prayer; and Maureen Greatrex, a young Anglican housewife from Cambridgeshire agreed to organise the following year's conference. The advisers, we agreed, should be increased by two, and they should not be Anglicans. We chose David Singleton and Brian Wills. That second national meeting was combined with a retreat led by the wonderful Cowley Father, Christopher Bryant.

And that set the pattern. Nearly every year there has been a national meeting, combined with a retreat led by people like Martin Israel, Robert Llewelyn and Mary Holliday. The Advisory Group grew gradually, and is now usually about nine or ten people. We try to keep a balance of male-female, clergy-lay, north-south, and of denominations.

The number of groups grew. Some met in churches, chapels or church rooms, but many in private homes. Some met weekly, some monthly, some fortnightly. Most were evening groups, but older people often arranged daytime ones. Some groups were formed in hospitals, prisons, schools.

Two remarkable Anglican priests were responsible for JM starting in other countries. After a long correspondence with Kevin Joyner in Australia the first JM groups started there in 1980, and spread to New Zealand in 1981. In that same year John Rowland began the first groups in South Africa. The United States took much longer. It wasn't until 1992 that an Episcopalian laywoman, Lynn Hay, inaugurated the first group there, which was in Illinois.

The Newsletter that we started with evolved into something called *The Julian Meeting Magazine*. It goes to all countries where there are groups, and each country inserts its own newsletter. For all but the first few years this international magazine has been edited by Pamela Fawcett.

The JM Ethos

Since there are only three criteria for Julian groups – that they be Christ-centred, based on contemplative prayer and at least potentially multi-denominational – they could in theory be very different from each other. No laws are laid down as to the structure of meetings: groups are encouraged to find out what is right for *them*. Yet most of them eventually move into a common pattern of starting with a brief reading, having half an hour's silence and ending with a prayer said together.

While most participants are aware that there are other groups nationally, or even in their own area, it is the local group – the increasingly-known, increasingly-trusted men and women in the group, and the support that they get and give – that is important to them.

All that is best about the movement comes, I am sure, from its mixture of denominations. Because the best Julian groups include not only lay people but clergy from various local churches there is not the usual expectation that 'the Vicar' or 'the Minister' will take the lead. Someone leads into the silence and out again at the end of the agreed time, but that will be a different person at each meeting, and will be randomly clerical or lay. Sometimes it comes as a surprise to clergy, how much they appreciate this opportunity to pray with others without having to lead. In some way connected with this playing down of differences, we tend not to use titles unless it is necessary. From fairly early on we have used just first name and surname. It's not a rule: it just seems to have happened and it feels right for us.

There are now nearly 300 JM groups in the United Kingdom. But there is no membership as such. Those who meet in the groups pay nothing, though they may be subscribers to *The Julian Meetings Magazine* which is available to anyone. Despite the original letter there is no badge or distinctive clothing. The movement has no headquarters, and owns no property.

The Advisory Group, which meets two or three times a year to make practical arrangements, keeps no minutes and has no elected officers: members are selected by taking on various short-term or long-term tasks, and working voluntarily and from home. At meetings of their local group they are ordinary participants.

But for many people what is most vital about the Julian Meetings, and the thing that differentiates them from other Christian meditation groups, is that they encourage those who are drawn to this way of prayer to find their *own way* into silence. To be restricted indefinitely to one particular technique is like being expected to live on baby food for ninety years. JM encourages people to know about different methods so that, not with flighty frequency but when they feel called to it, they can move to a different approach.

Misconceptions and Realities

Since this whole book is about contemplative prayer, it may seem superfluous to attempt a basic statement about what it is. But there are some odd misconceptions around that it would be good to clear up.

The worst misconception is that contemplation is 'letting the Devil in'. I have heard one or two ministers say this and I have been appalled to think that they are depriving their people of a very deep experience of the presence of God through their own ignorance or fear. No prayer offered to God, no heart opened to God, can be said to produce evil. I believe that this thinking comes from the experience that some have, when the mind is cleared of all that we so deliberately keep it full of, of thoughts surfacing that have been long repressed. They surface precisely because they have not been dealt with. The solution is to bring them into God's light and allow God to heal us of whatever they represent: pains and griefs, intolerable desires, or that side of ourselves which we know to be not altogether good.

Another misconception is that contemplative prayer is difficult, and only for those who can give many hours to it. Anyone can do it. Children can. Many of us can remember engaging in it as children, though we wouldn't have given it a name or thought we were doing anything in particular. And the adults around us would probably not have known what we were doing, or that they may unknowingly have helped by providing the surroundings that made it possible: quiet churches, chapels, the open countryside, the sea.

Although many books have been written about it, contemplative prayer is very simple: a stilling of the mind and body to attend to God. All we need is a desire for God, for a closer relationship with God. And then amazingly God seems to do the rest: entices, rewards, draws us on, delights and encourages us. So that it is not a duty or a chore but something we turn to very willingly – because it is deeply pleasurable. Wherever did we get the idea that we are not to enjoy God?

To anyone who has never tried to meditate the bare statement that anyone can do it may be rather annoying. And so, for anyone who wants to begin, I offer this basic lead-in. Find somewhere where you will be undisturbed. Sit comfortably upright. Decide how long you will spend in silence – probably no more than five or ten minutes to begin with – and commit that time to God. Consciously relax your body, and let your breathing flow gently but from right down in your diaphragm rather than your chest. Be aware of all that your senses tell you: what you can see, smell, hear, taste, feel. Choose a God-centring word or phrase to take into the silence, close your eyes and begin not just to think it, but to say it in your mind, over and over again, gently and in time with your breathing, until it becomes drowned in silence. Be as still as you can, so that your body can find its own unity and your mind and your heart can enter that unity. You will not need to try to be conscious of God: you have put yourself into God's keeping and that is enough. When your time is up mark the end of your silence by a brief prayer or a physical movement such as a sign of the cross or a bow of gratitude.

What happens between the beginning and the end of your meditation will range from being indescribable to being boring. It may seem as if you have spent the time fighting off intrusive trivial thoughts or deeper anxieties or concerns. A good way of dealing with them is to recognise them and give them over to God on the understanding that you will retrieve them and deal with them later: and thus to go back into stillness. On some occasions you may experience a timelessness, an evenness quite featureless and yet sensed as containing all that is, from which you emerge with a calm joy, refreshed and recreated. No matter how the time of meditation is felt, it is always a precious exchange: your gift to God, God's gift to you.

Once you know that you want to pray this way it is important to decide how long and how often you will do it – and stick to it. Too short a time is better than an ambitious length that you will constantly fall.

With time the practice changes us. We recognise it ourselves, or others notice it. They comment that we are less grumbly or less uptight, more patient or more fair-minded. As we change for the better the world changes for the better. Practitioners of Transcendental Meditation reckon they can cut the crime rate in a given area if they can get ten per cent of the population meditating. Soka Gakkai Buddhists are, at the time I write this, chanting (arguably a form of meditation) for peace in Ireland and democracy in South Africa. Cynics will deny that meditation can have any effect on the social problems of the world. Yet even if we take the popular butterfly theory (that a butterfly moving its wings in Beijing can alter the climate in California) as no more than a pictorial way of saying that everything that happens affects the future of everything else, how can we doubt that millions of people engaging in a selfless state of good will can affect the state of the world?

To join occasionally with other people who meditate can be a great encouragement, especially after the first flush of enthusiasm. At first it feels different to be in such utter silence with other people if you have been accustomed to meditating on your own, but then it becomes very precious and valuable. And your daily solo meditations are then upheld by the knowledge that those others are also praying in this way in their own daily routines.

Every day of the week, every day of the month – with the probable exception of Sundays and days like Christmas – Julian groups are meeting somewhere, together keeping a silence of rapt attention to God, and ensuring that every day of the year – without any exceptions – those thousands of people, people of every variety, alone or together, are turning to God in the contemplation that is beyond words and that daily brings the world and God closer together.

The Future

This book marks our twenty-first anniversary. In one sense this saddens me. I wrote in our magazine on our tenth anniversary that I hoped we would not reach our twentieth. What I meant was that I hoped that by then the prayer of silence would have become such a normal part of Christian life that there would no longer be any need for a network like JM. That hasn't happened, yet there still seems ground for hope that it will. More and more, people are asking for periods of silence during their church services. Increasingly the wonder of silence is experienced at places like Taizé, or on parish 'quiet days', or during a few days away at a retreat house.

When this movement first started most of us felt that attitudes to praying were polarized, with on the one extreme those who were drawn to the prayer of silence and on the other those who prayed charismatically. Over the years, people have come to feel much freer about using both ways. Now we are enriched by being able to pray in many different ways.

But there are still far too many people who have never experienced either way of praying let alone both. There is still a sadly prevalent assumption that being a Christian is about going to church on Sundays, and striving to be good the rest of the week. That's like getting married without being in love. The desire to worship God and to live in union with God – to be 'good' – flows naturally from the experience of God: but many need to be encouraged to allow themselves that experience.

Maybe the Julian Meetings and other such movements still need to grow.

Hilary Wakeman describes herself as the inadvertent founder of the Julian Meetings. Be that as it may, she has been its guide and inspiration from the start. She is an Anglican priest working in the Diocese of Norwich.

Prayer and Theology

A. M. ALLCHIN

One of the most striking signs that we *are* living in a time when there is a rapidly increasing interest in prayer and spirituality is the growth in interest in Julian of Norwich. Since 1973, the sixth centenary of Julian's revelations of Christ which led to *The Revelations of Divine Love*, when there were celebrations in Norwich and the first Julian meetings were founded, every year has seen new evidence of how Julian and her teaching has become living in our time. There have been films and broadcasts, big scholarly books and small popular books. People have come to Norwich to visit her shrine as individual pilgrims, and they have come in groups large and small. It is clear from many points of view that people find Julian fascinating. But, one cannot help asking, where does all this increase of interest lead? How can we avoid it burning itself out in mere enthusiasm, or a passing fashion?

For me the answer to that question was given at the time when I was first beginning to think about the Christian faith more than forty years ago. There can be no true theology without spirituality, experience, mysticism. But there can be no true Christian spirituality or mysticism without theology, the loving contemplation of the great central truths of the

Christian mystery. These two convictions I learned from two contrasting authors, one Anglican, the other Orthodox; Fr R. M. Benson and Vladimir Lossky. It so happens that both men have been the subject of studies which seem to expound their relevance for the present day; Benson is the subject of a book of essays edited by Fr Martin Smith SSJE and called simply *Benson of Cowley* (Oxford University Press). Lossky is the underlying influence in my own book *The Kingdom of Love and Knowledge* (Darton, Longman and Todd) and the last essay in the book consists of a brief study of his thought.

For both Benson and Lossky, one in Victorian Oxford, the other in twentieth-century Paris, it is evident that the apophatic principle is vital for all sane theology, for all healthy thought and talk about God. That is the principle which acknowledges the radical inadequacy of all human words and concepts before the infinite mystery of God. God always transcends utterly all that we could say or think or experience of him. We come to know him, not in the abstract at a distance, but by coming into relationship with him, by allowing ourselves to be drawn into communion with him, a communion of love no less than of knowledge, a communion in which silence has an even more fundamental role than speech.

Seen in this light the truths of our faith become active powers of life. 'Those truths which Divine revelation sets before us are not abstract considerations but active energies with which we must co-operate', writes Fr Benson. And again, 'The contemplation of theological mysteries is the very foundation of that practical life of holiness whereby we are to appropriate the gift of Divine joy'.

In this kind of perspective, as I try to show in the opening chapters of *The Kingdom of Love and Knowledge*, many of the theological controversies of the last thirty years or so look strangely familiar. 'Our image of God must go' was one of the messages of John Robinson's *Honest to God* in the Sixties. But of course, *all* images of God must in the end go, be transcended as we enter into union with God himself in Jesus Christ. It is not a matter of choosing one image rather than another, such as 'God within us' rather than 'God beyond', or 'the Divine depth' rather than 'the Divine height'. It is rather a matter of seeing something about the nature of *all* our words and concepts and images, recognising the priority of silence and amazement, obedience and love.

Hence the recovery of a true and healing theology is intimately linked with the recovery of the true practice of prayer, personal and corporate, silent and spoken, informal and liturgical. Only out of an atmosphere of prayer will it be possible to understand the words of theology in a creative and healing way. All our speech about God needs to be rooted in our speech with God, and that in turn needs to be rooted in a silence and a receptivity in which we learn that it is God who speaks first and that it is our part to respond to him.

When this is not the case we are always tempted to speak of God in 'a way which will enable us to make use of Him, or to speak dominatingly or condescendingly of him to others. As soon as we do this, theological language begins to go bad on us, to lose its true content and significance. For it is a language which must be rooted in the experience and reality of worship' (*The Kingdom of Love and Knowledge*, page 5).

The present concerns with spirituality, with the rediscovery of the inner life, is something of very great promise. But it needs to be linked with a rediscovery of the central affirmations of Christian faith, so that the inner and the outer may be joined together, so that the personal experience of each may find its foundation and fulfilment in the corporate tradition of faith and experience which the Christian centuries can convey to us.

Seen in this way the recovery of the way of prayer and meditation will be found to be at the centre of the whole movement for Christian unity and reconciliation, as also of the beginnings of a new relationship between Christians and men and women of other faiths.

Canon A. M. Allchin is Director of the St Theosevia Centre, Oxford. He is the author of *Praise above All* (University of Wales Press, 1991) and *The Joy of All Creation: An Anglican Meditation on the Place of Mary* (New City, 1994).

Contemplative Prayer: a Brief Glimpse
JOHN ALLEN

Perhaps it isn't so surprising that more and more people who are aware of a religious dimension in their lives are increasingly expressing the wish to know something about contemplative prayer.

This wish no doubt springs from an uneasy feeling that the kind of prayers they have been taught and tried to practise sometimes seem a little unreal. Prayer has been felt to be a duty and obligation fulfilled through the performance of a kind of 'prayer drill'. There seems so much that ought to be done: thanking, confessing and endless intercession. This dutiful approach to God has, for many, become impersonal.

Moreover if we face up to reality, we become a little uneasy. In what seems to be our weaker moments we are tempted to ask the faithless question: 'does prayer make any difference?' We go on praying for Europe and the rest of the world and for reconciliation in Northern Ireland. We pray for one thing, but our experience of the world we live in prepares us to expect the other. When we pray do we have to suspend our normal intelligence? Or do we pray with our 'tongue in our cheek'?

Such doubts and questions are regarded as right and normal in our world today. We are taught to question everything. Yet to question the validity and authenticity of prayer comes dangerously near to undermining the practice of prayer. So we either refuse to face up to the issue and try to live with a foot in both camps or we give up altogether. Many people can't make up their minds and end up with a tepid, unreal prayer life and a guilty conscience.

For such people contemplative prayer often comes as a joyous surprise. It is a way of escape, a release from the paraphernalia of trying to 'say your prayers'. We can liken ourselves to a child who has been shut up in a stuffy classroom trying in vain to master the lesson. The child is released and allowed to run freely through the fields, and a new insight and awareness dawns. The child is not so dull after all. In this new atmosphere of freedom the child at last finds his true life.

But what is contemplative prayer? Quite simply, it is a gift. Somebody may be struggling with their prayers when God seems to interrupt and tell them to be quiet, and to be still. 'Stop trying so hard'. God places his finger on our lips. He restrains us from all our restless activity.

It is when we are still that we begin to become alive. It is possible to live in a place and be among people and yet never see or hear. We are so concerned with our pounding preoccupations that our perception of the reality all round us is blunted, our sensitivity deadened. It is useful just to be in a place and allow ourselves to be receptive.

This comes as the gift of life to people, bringing them refreshment and a new awareness of God, themselves, the people and the world around them. It is the well of water within which is a spring bubbling up to give life in all its fullness. Such prayer is not escapist in the bad sense of the word. It is rather an escape from the restrictions of our artificial schemes and methods into a real world of incredible possibility.

What I have said is just a glimpse of a dimension of life which is opened up for so many people by what we call contemplative prayer. This is no esoteric skill for the favoured few, rather it is the discovery of a truly religious life right in the heart of our own being, and in the very centre of our present situation and circumstances.

John Allen is Warden to the Sisters at East Grinstead and Rector of St Nicholas, Chislehurst, Kent.

Second Tuesday

JOHN APPLEYARD

> Moving from the solitary
> To community:
> The one with others,

Facing Him who is other
Yet intimately ours.
Self facing selves,
Gathered to wait on God.

How odd that in the silence
Friendship grows apace
Before the face
Of burning Spirit
Who consumes our enmity,
Making God's celebrity
Known among His people.
Those varied souls whose roles
Present a spectrum of belief,
Tradition and the common bond
To each other in the fond
Remembrance of Dame Julian's name.

None who meet
For this retreat
Will ever be the same.
Blessed are those who come
On the second Tuesday
Of the month to wait
Upon the Lord, the Son.

Prayer as an Offering

ELIZABETH BASSET

'Lord let me offer you in sacrifice the service of my thoughts and my tongue, but first give me what I may offer to you.'

This prayer of St Augustine seems to me to be the only way in which one can dare speak or write of the deep things of the spirit. One fears to trample clumsily on mysteries 'too deep for words'. So often I have found that when trying to put feelings into words something is lost, some secret mystery one has cherished is changed. Mercifully there are those who have the great gift of being able to communicate the deep things without anything being lost or changed. At the same time there is a great need to share the joys and sorrows of those things which we find so hard to put into words and perhaps the only way to overcome this difficulty is by the offering to God that which he has first given to us.

Words are necessary. How poor we should be without the enrichment of our literature, of our poetry and how grateful we are to those writers and poets who have shared their insights and inspirations with us and with, who knows what, cost to themselves. We also have the tradition of the mystics in their silent contemplation and which of us has not benefited by the silence after listening to a reading or a prayer or music?

I like so much a passage taken from Robert Llewelyn's *With Pity Not With Blame*, where he is talking about the time set apart for prayer.

> It will probably be a recurring temptation to end before the time is up. This is likely to be because it seems that nothing is happening, and that we are simply wasting our time. . . What can be helpful in the presence of this temptation is to see one's prayer as an *offering*. About an offering there are two important points. One is that it shall be given gladly, willingly and lovingly, and the other is that it doesn't matter whether it succeeds or not in the ordinary sense in which we use that dubious word. An offering has simply to be offered, and we should despise all thoughts such as whether our prayer is strengthening to ourselves or to anybody else. We simply make it as best we can, a free response to the grace given us - for God does not override our freedom - through the Holy Spirit. And as we make it - it may help to reflect - not alone but in union with the whole Body of Christ, in both this life and the life beyond.

This is summed up in Susan Wood's poem.

> How can I say it?
> How can a word
> Be made to bear
> So great a weight?
>
> And yet, the poem done,
> A paper boat
> Upon a glittering sea,
> My hurt is gone
>
> Out of me, out of me.

I once read of a man who said it had suddenly dawned upon him that it was not his ability but his availability that God wanted of him. This I have found most comforting on the many occasions when ability has been in short supply! It is perhaps in the prayer of silence that we can be most available. We can be so in listening, in stillness, in loving attention; to God, to each other, to the world in the sense that through making ourselves available, God can use this to work out his purposes for the world. In some mysterious way we can become the link in the chain of God's love, reaching out to all those in such desperate need of His love. Reaching out to all those *we* love and care about and who of ourselves we seem so powerless to help.

When we are most aware of the inadequacy of our prayer life and are tempted over and over again to give up the battle, the advice given by

Evelyn Underhill in her *Necessity for Prayer* is most helpful in showing us that the efficacy of our prayer does not depend on ourselves alone, that when it seems most dead and hopeless it may be that the Holy Spirit of God is doing it for us, using our availability even though we feel nothing.

> Do not entertain the notion that you ought to advance in your prayer. If you do you will only find you have put on the brake instead of the accelerator. All real progress in spiritual things comes quietly, imperceptibly, and it is the work of God. Our crude efforts spoil it. Know yourself for the childish, limited and dependent soul you are. Remember that the only growth which matters happens without our knowledge and that trying to stretch ourselves is both dangerous and silly. Think of the Infinite Goodness, never of your own state. Realise that the very capacity to pray at all is the free gift of the Divine Love, and be content with St Francis de Sales' favourite prayer in which all personal religion is summed up: 'Yes Father, Yes and always Yes!
>
> Let us rejoice in the great adoring acts and splendid heroisms of God's great Lovers and humbly do the little bit we can. We too have our place.

Lady Elizabeth Basset is Lady-in-Waiting to HM Queen Elizabeth the Queen Mother. She has edited three well-known anthologies, and her fourth is *Interpreted by Love* (Darton, Longman & Todd, 1994).

The Struggle for Silence

DAVID BENTLEY

It is an odd experience to be sitting in a train which for no apparent reason stops between stations. The noise from the wind and the wheels dies down and a stillness descends upon all the passengers. Conversation that was being conducted quite loudly some moments before, now becomes subdued and self-conscious. The silence is uncomfortable. We have been caught off our guard and we feel strangely defenceless. We feel a sudden need to do something; to cough or blow our nose, to stare at the newspaper which we have already thoroughly read – anything to fill the emptiness of the moment. When at last the train moves off and noise again fills the carriage, the relief is almost tangible.

We all have an awkward relationship with silence. It attracts us, yet quickly eludes us. We protest loudly that all we want is a bit of peace and quiet, but when we get an unexpected hour of space, we quickly look for something to fill it. Even in our churches we speak about the need for silence far more than we actually allow it. More than once I have caught myself taking longer over the introduction to a time of silence than over the actual silence itself!

I think we are undoubtedly double-minded when it comes to being still.

Our lives have many such contradictions. We complain of too many demands, yet become very uneasy when no more are made. We speak of the burden of letter-writing, yet hate it when we receive no mail. We look with anticipation to the pleasures of retirement, but dread the day when it will arrive. In short, while desiring to be alone, we are frightened of being alone. Perhaps it is because our struggle with silence is a struggle with our own identity. So we keep nice and busy, we fill up our diaries with lots of lovely engagements and we manage to justify our lives with what we think of as success and achievement. And, if we are not very careful, action crowds out reflection – and I believe we need proper reflection if our actions are to be worthwhile.

Of all places, it ought to be the church where such reflection can take place, where there need be no guilt about taking lots of time and space to be still. It is built deeply into our Biblical tradition and indeed into the development of monastic life and of religious communities: 'Jesus withdrew to a place apart . . . when you pray, go into your secret chamber and shut the door . . . Be still and know that I am God.'

Yet I wonder how many of us build into our daily and annual programmes vital times of space and silence, so that this reflection can take place? I read somewhere that silence is a great leveller. You certainly discover that very quickly when you are on retreat. Silence there humbles the eloquent and exalts the tongue-tied. It allows no one to dominate and no one to be dominated. There is a true equality to be discovered, a spiritual order to be found in the fellowship of silence. It brings a new sensitivity to those around us. It brings a new gentleness with which we can truly love each other. Silence teaches us to love people for who they are, not for the clever things they say.

We must all learn a new pace of living. We need to create the space within our churches that will encourage the call to stillness before God. We are not good at listening – we do not easily learn to listen to the Lord. I believe the better use of silence is the beginning of such listening. It is, of course, easy to write about but not nearly so easy to put into practice. But, if we can make our churches much more than they are into centres of stillness, if we can enable our public worship to be surrounded much more than it is with silence and recollection, then I believe many more will find within Christian worship that essential core of inner stability for which so many hunger today.

David Bentley is Bishop of Gloucester and was formerly Bishop of Lynn.

Words and THE WORD

IVY BISHOP

> Too many words!
> THE WORD lost in a sea of words.
> 'In the beginning was THE WORD!'
> But where is it now?
>
> So many words
> To explain one WORD
> Written and spoken and thought
> Until THE WORD is buried in words
> So that some say
> There is no WORD
>
> So I offer you, Lord
> My silence
> And in the silence
> You alone shall teach me.
> Teach me the WORD
> And I will live it.
>
> What greater thing
> Can I do for your world
> Than ponder your WORD
> And try to live it?
> For THE WORD WAS MADE FLESH
> AND DWELT AMONG US.

Ivy Bishop shares in the ministry of her husband Bishop Jim Bishop (retired), and is an active member of her group of parishes, the Deanery Synod, Mother's Union and the ecumenical Focolare Movement.

God Did Not Say

FRANCIS BOSTON

> God did not say
> You will find me
> if you carry out
> a deep enough analysis.
>
> God did not say
> I have made a tree

To know me
you must
cut it down,
cut it up
pulp it
make paper
and write upon it
Holy Words.

God did not say
I have made a butterfly
Don't let it flutter by
Get it
Net it
Set it
and hold it up
dead
in praise of me

God did not say
anything.
Silently
He made
all things
all stones
all plants
all flowers
all animals
and man
as One.
And
without loudspeakers
without book
without script
without word,
without letter,
even without
a Little Bang Theory –
and God saw
that it was Good.
Perhaps
we should.

Music and Contemplation

LYNNE BROUGHTON

Not long ago I had a minor accident in my car (the other driver's fault, of course!). The car was badly dented; my neck received a nasty jolt. The best treatment for this was to lie flat on my back for an hour or so at intervals during the day. I could not even read a book because holding it would put strain on the neck. What a boring waste of time in a busy life! As a Julian member I was used to periods of silence but somehow these times of enforced rest were not conducive to prayer in themselves, without some help.

Fortunately a few weeks previously I had been reading Jaroslav Pelikan's book *Bach Among the Theologians*.[1] It had been clear to me for some years that Bach was indeed a great theologian but here his theology was spelt out in fascinating detail. Some recordings of Bach cantatas I already had; others were borrowed from the local library and it was a rare luxury to be able to listen with total attention to the greatest of Christian composers. Indeed it was a compelling lead-in to meditation and contemplation. Many prayer groups start with a reading and a piece of music – which are often not related to one another. But here the two were fully integrated and could provide for others, too, either a preparation for contemplative prayer or, if that is what is needed, solid food for meditation.

Now the very name of Bach can put you off as sounding too heavy and too difficult. Some background knowledge is needed in order to grasp what Bach is doing and be able to enjoy his music. If you are attracted by the idea but do not know where and how to begin perhaps the following brief introduction may help you.

Bach was a Lutheran, writing, playing and conducting for Lutheran church services. Unlike most of the other Protestant reformers, Luther considered music to be not just an optional ornament but essential nourishment for the life of the spirit. 'After theology', he said, 'I give music the highest place and highest honour. The notes bring the text to life.'

So Bach was working within a tradition in which music was highly honoured and had an essential part to play in the regular Sunday services. This music took the form both of congregational hymns and also of more complex, sophisticated music for choir, soloists and instruments. The latter, those pieces now known as cantatas, oratorios and passions, were written for a particular liturgical purpose: to be performed at the main Sunday services before and sometimes also after the sermon.

The texts were based on the readings proper to the day. They made much use of the words of scripture in meditation upon the day's theme and tended to be structured along the lines of the classic systems of meditation. So the music needed to reflect the meaning of the words, to underline, enliven and perhaps also comment upon them. The congregations were provided with printed texts so that they could join their own prayer and meditation with the music that was being performed. Bach used every means at his disposal to interpret the words, so that we might be not merely instructed but moved and transformed by the Christian message they contain.

Some people find Bach's music hard to enjoy because they think of it as 'heavy'. This, I think, is due to having heard only those performances of a previous generation which used unsuitable instruments and where the assumption seems to have been that religious music must always be slow and solemn. Yet Bach was reported by one of his sons as generally playing his music at a lively tempo. In view of this, most modern 'authentic' performances tend to be livelier, lighter and faster than the older interpretations.[2]

Another reason why Bach's music is thought of as solemn is that his Passions are the most frequently performed of his religious works. Their concentration of the suffering and death of Christ requires a certain solemnity of tone. Yet many of the cantatas are based, as is only right, on the psalms of praise. These cantatas tend to make much use of dance rhythms, insistent and joyful invitations to the everlasting delights of heaven where, as Dante suggests, the blessed spend their eternity carolling – that is, dancing and singing with joy.

My favourite of these praising cantatas is no. 134, which consists almost entirely of such skipping, infectious dance music. But I have chosen as most suitable to begin silent prayer one of Bach's cantatas for solo voice. If you do not already know this music, I suggest that it is a good idea to play it through several times so that it becomes familiar. Try putting it on as background music while cooking or driving.

Cantata No. 170 is known as *Vergnügte Ruh* (O blessed peace) from the first words of the first section.[3] It is written for contralto, organ and small orchestra; with only one singing voice it is a personal, intimate work. The text is based on the Epistle to the Romans (6:3-11) and St Matthew's Gospel (5:20-26). It might be helpful to read one or both of these Bible passages when using the cantata to lead into prayer.

In the first section the words reflect on how the soul longs for peace but cannot find it here on earth. This is sung to a gentle, meditative melody, as though the soul is trying to rock itself into the desired peace. Then in a short interlude, accompanied only by a harpsichord, the voice tells of how it is sin that makes rest impossible, because sinners seek, not the will of God, but hatred and revenge. The effects of this are enacted in the central section. Here organ, orchestra and voice wander off on their separate ways, sometimes clashing in dissonant sounds, never really in harmony. The organ is the last to finish: it has won the battle but without much glory. In this whole section the music lacks a bass part; it is missing what is technically known as a *ground bass*. Now Bach certainly knew of the traditional description of God as 'The Ground of Being'. Here he is deliberately illustrating what it feels, and sounds, like to cut ourselves off from our natural foundation in God.

There follows another short interlude (a *recitative*) with the singer accompanied only by the harpsichord. Here the words begin with a reflection on the sorry effects of sin, but then modulate towards the statement that in Christ sin has been overcome, so that through faith and hope in him the soul can be led to the heavenly Jerusalem.

Bliss and joy are the theme of the final section where organ, orchestra and voice (complete with bass line) join together in perfect harmony. All conflict is resolved and the organ embroiders upon the vocal melody with a series of little chuckling phrases as if unable to contain its delight in reconciliation. And if one moves into silent prayer with this skipping tune singing in one's head, what better mantra could there be to occupy the mind and imagination while the will stays intent on God?

As Bach wrote in the margin of his bible: 'In devotional music, God with His grace is always present.'

1. Jaroslav Pelikan, *Bach Among the Theologians* (Fortress Press, Philadelphia, 1986).
2. For this newer, more authentic style of performing Bach, look for recordings on which Nikolaus Harnoncourt, Gustav Leonhardt, Joshua Rifkin or John Eliot Gardner are conducting.
3. Several good recordings are available, including one with Dame Janet Baker and The Academy of St Martin in the Fields, conducted by Sir Neville Marriner on Teldoc.

Lynne Broughton is an Associate Lecturer in the Divinity Faculty of the University of Cambridge, and a lecturer at Lincoln Theological College. For many years she has been a Companion of the (Anglican) Society of the Precious Blood, and she conducts retreats making use of Bach's music.

On Seeing the Frink Madonna in Salisbury Close

HEATHER BUCK

> She will not wait for me.
> No longer bound in alcoves
> of the mind or in the naves
> of tall cathedrals, she strides
> her independence as the air,

her flying skirts dispersing
dust layered images.

All time has made her wait,
a glitter of candles at her feet,
hearing the heavy door stun
noises from the street,
her stage paste effigy
provoking dumb confusions
and prayers that falter
on a rack of doubt.

Now she leads along untrodden tracks.
Suffering has mapped her face
and gulleys of pain
have seamed that country.
Compassion is no stranger there

but even so a knot
of tributaries about the eyes
is fed by laughter.
A thousand shadows at her back – in front
purpose breaks from her like light.

Distractions

HEATHER BUCK

Summer devours us with distractions,
As near as the shrub-rose at the door,
The hub-hub in the hall.

But when the wounded sun lies in the earth,
And snow is being unskeined from the sky
In fold after fold,
There is time to contemplate the winter
In solitudes of snow,
In the necessary distance of the human voice,
In the silence of the empty hall.

Wanting solitude so long, strange to find silence
Itself so noisy with sound. Does the ear seek
The wind's complaint under the door,
The little draught playing in the chandelier?
Is it fear that twitches and writhes
In the shadows, furnishes
The dark corner of the hall with threats?

And afterwards there's the inner debate.
Silence made loud with interminable discourse,
Nowhere to escape the trivial I chattering,
No landscape inviolate from the tip
Of one's own smouldering rubbish.

Perhaps only the privileged find it.
The mystic's void scraped clear to a flawless
Perfection. Or the tortured few
In their suffering's grossest extremity
Find they're no longer alone.

Heather Buck has written many poems and is the author of *At the Window* (Anvil Press Poetry).

From the Cradle to Contemplation

HILARY BURN

There comes a time when the prayers of childhood and the early days are not adequate and the prayerful person needs to reach out to other prayers. But what other prayers? Most of us need to be shown how to pray.

My own need came very late, I now realise, when traditional prayers and extempore prayers were not enough. They had nothing to say to me, I was not able to hear God speak because of the words which were getting in the space between Him and me. I sensed a reaching out to me, but was not able to hear what was being said. The Charismatic approach came my way, and I was encouraged and led into the joyful uplifting of prayer and the reaching-out to God in praise and excitement. It was still not what I was seeking, but a friend who was a Sister in a nearby convent understood and pointed me to a contemplative prayer meeting – a Julian Meeting. Here I found in contemplation that the voice of God could be heard. The clatter of life – the noise and the other voices were set aside and in the silence God was there.

Silent prayer isn't an immediate answer; it is not the cure-all for our ills and needs. It has to be explored and learnt one step at a time. There are many, many times of silence when nothing seems to happen. One can sit in the right atmosphere, in the right frame of mind and in the right fellowship, and yet not seem to hear the words of God. It sometimes seems that He is not there and the time is wasted. This is not so. Even times where not a single feeling of God's presence is there, even this time is well-used, because you have sat in the knowledge of God and turned your heart to Him.

There is so much God can do in a life turned to Him. To find out if this is the path He has for you, you need to put yourself in His presence, in silence, and maybe the answer will come clearly. Yet God uses many paths and your life may be led steadily in a way you had not thought to follow. Perseverance is a great virtue. When you feel you are not getting anywhere in your search for God, that is the time to persevere – regular and faithful times of contemplation, can bring the reward as God uses your attentive heart.

Many people find the use of a mantra helps them. A word or phrase which is used repetitively may still the surface of the mind, while you prepare for silence in the presence of God. This is only a tool, used by those who find distractions fill every corner of a busy mind, and it can be put to one side when contemplation becomes more familiar. Make no mistake, just sitting and thinking about God gives the opportunity for a multitude of thoughts to butt in and distract you! A mantra occupies the surface of your thoughts and gives the busy part of the brain something specific to do and allows God to penetrate your being with His presence. A word or phrase or quotation from the Bible can be used as a mantra. The Jesus Prayer can also be used with great benefit. 'Lord Jesus Christ - Son of God - Have mercy on me'. Just the name, Lord Jesus Christ, will help to keep our thoughts on God. However, the use of silence is not that we are thinking of God. It is that we are putting ourselves in the presence of God, and in that presence God can speak and we will hear. And hopefully we will understand.

We are all too eager to do what we can, to speak, to reach out, to influence. Yet it is much more important that we make ourselves the least important part of the prayer time and that we place ourselves within God's loving presence. God is the centre, the all-important, the one who acts, speaks and influences through us. He must be the greatest, we are the least.

It is in this attitude that we can use the silence, and be used by God.

Let it not be thought that this is an easy way of prayer. It is simple because it is easily stated and understood; it takes no special words, no special equipment is required, no particular place or time. But it is not easy; it can seem to be laborious. When we start perhaps we are tempted to feel that there are no results, and that nothing can be achieved this way. We don't have to achieve anything. God can use us and the achievements are His. We cannot remain the same person if we really set ourselves to pray in a contemplative way. God changes us and uses what He wants from us and from that time on, we change. New challenges lie ahead. New ways we have never dreamt of are before us; new faith; new service. Those who seek God rarely fail to find Him. He is ever ready to stretch out to each one of us. The only thing we have to do is put ourselves, with true humility and love, in His presence.

And leave it all to Him.

Hilary Burn is a Lay Preacher and an Elder in the United Reformed Church. She is treasurer of Julian Meetings and a member of the Advisory Group.

The Vision of God

JOHN BYROM

'We grow by attention', says Iris Murdoch in *The Sovereignty of Good*, 'attention is our daily bread'. Not that religion is a matter of self-culture, or anything so dreary. It is the desire of God himself that all should know him. And the achievement - though that isn't the right word because it is mainly a gift - of the vision of God is the only thing that lends authenticity, meaning and direction to the whole paraphernalia of what goes under the name of organised religion. It is the whole point of prayer, which is itself the heart of religion. 'I sought my God', Augustine said, 'that if possible I might not only believe but actually see something.' So as a focus for thought may I offer that great cry of Moses, 'I beseech thee, show me thy glory', taking glory here to mean all that God is in his concentrated essence.

At the beginning of the Christian era preoccupation with such vision was very marked and widespread, producing epoch-making writing; Philonic, Hermetic, Rabbinic, and so on. 'The world', says K. E. Kirk in his Bampton lectures of 1928, 'was not unprepared for the (Church's) message (of the vision of God); indeed it was the one message for which the whole world, Jewish and Greek alike, was waiting.'

Through A Glass Darkly

What is meant by seeing God? There is at least one strand in Old Testament teaching which says that no man shall see God and live; and while it is still true for us living under the New Covenant, in another sense that tradition has been modified. For we have, I still believe, seen God in the face of Jesus. God means to be seen, but indirectly, through a glass darkly, because anything more direct would destroy our sight. So that Jesus really functions in two ways: refracting the glare, and focussing the immensity. He is in fact the point where the Vision of God comes into focus.

But what sort of thing is this vision? It is first dim, 'a dim yet direct perception', in Cuthbert Butler's famous phrase; or in Bishop Hedley's classic description, 'a spreading, silent, sense of something near at hand, vague in outline, colourless and dim, accompanied by burning love.' The young French nun Elizabeth of the Trinity said 'It is an encounter face to face in darkness'; rather, I imagine, like a blind man's awareness of his wife.

It consists of feeling, awareness, background knowledge, proved experience, every kind of aesthetic sensitivity and, as the hymn says, all this 'warmed by love'; indeed it is the addition of love, as in the experience of falling in love, that fuses these scattered perceptions into a single track of intuitive sight. 'My mind in the flash of a trembling glance came to that which is,' (that is, to God;) so said Augustine.

And yet, paradoxically, not much of a coherent nature can be said about the actual business of seeing; not because the object is unreal or insubstantial, but precisely because it is so real and concentrated. 'God himself', von Hügel said, 'is a stupendously rich reality.'

Just as films and plays in bygone less sophisticated days used to work up to, and find their meaning in, the magic moment when two people realised their love and declared it, but couldn't go any further because everything starts all over again from here, so not much can be said, anyhow coherently, about this interior sense of the Father's presence. It can't be talked about satisfactorily just because it is so concentrated, and at the same time so wordless that it contains and covers everything that can be said, and nothing except the utterances of Jesus himself can plumb its depths, and even they leave us peering into infinity. 'There's something fishy about describing other people's feelings', Iris Murdoch says. 'For most of us truth can be attained, if at all, only in silence.'

This is why the key figures of the Old and New Testaments are regularly reduced to silence: not the silence of vacancy but incoherent stupefaction in the presence of an overwhelming concentration of truth and reality, or reality of truth. They are only moments, but they are worth all the other long diluted hours of the day, and indeed make those hours possible and meaningful. A normal marriage, after all, is fed by, and revolves around, swift moments of speechless intensity of communion, and so does the soul's existence on this side of death.

Blessed Are The Pure In Heart

How then is this vision, this awareness, to be come by? First it is, because it has to be, essentially a gift from God himself. God is not like a pop-star whom you have to fight to get a view of. Religion, as I said, is not self-culture, though often confused with it. It is a means of bringing us to God, who anyhow wants to disclose himself. There is therefore no merit in achieving it, though tragedy in missing it. It is everyone's destiny.

Secondly, an element of moral purity is involved. Any sort of life won't do. Mere intellect won't do. 'There is no seeing God as he is except by becoming like him': so said Bishop Rust in 1667. Likewise, do look at what Iris Murdoch has to say about the purification of our sight through attention to her essays in *The Sovereignty of Good.*

The condition of vision is always righteousness. 'The upright shall behold his face' is the proper translation of the last words of Psalm 11; and Kirk quotes a Rabbinic comment on Ezekiel 11:19 to the effect that 'he whose stony heart has become flesh is worthy to look upon the face of the Shekinah'. 'Only the pure may touch the pure', Plato said. Seneca, the Roman dramatist and moralist and St Paul's contemporary, can say in one of his letters: 'The mind, unless it is pure and holy, cannot apprehend God.' And of course, supremely, the words of Jesus, 'Blessed are the pure in heart, for they shall see God'. And there is nothing in the New Testament to suggest that this vision is limited to life after death. Indeed, all evidence of Christian spirituality suggests it is a possibility and a fact of experience now.

By purity I mean what has been described as 'the simplicity of an undivided will', an undivided, loyal, heroic submission to the truth as one sees it in the conscience and intellect combined; and as F. J. A. Hort said in his Hulsean lectures of 1871, 'a life devoted to truth is a life of vanities abased and ambitions forsworn', since it is precisely the idolatrous vanities and ambitions of men which block the vision.

The Crown Of All Knowledge

The path to vision, once this moral aspect of obedience has been grasped, is by way of each and every branch of knowledge. God cannot be fully known except by a patient study of his own creation. 'He who loves nothing else but God', Hort says with tremendous power, 'destroys the possibility of loving God, for the universe is the remoter and diffracted utterance of Christ', God's master-workman and instrument in creation.

But in the last analysis you come to the vision of God through Christ, the image of God. Yet there is no break between Christ and creation because, as that great man Hort says again, 'no truth can be alien to him who is the truth'. We don't study Christ and creation with different spectacles but with the same total humility because Christ himself is the crown of creation, sending rays of brilliance into every part of it. Therefore, as old Jeremy Taylor said, nothing can be found to be true which is unholy. And to quote Hort again, 'the gospel itself can never be fully known till nature as well as man is fully known'. We humans don't live in a spiritual vacuum. Even our bodies are a way into the mystery: even physical beauty is a valid route, 'mere side-reverse of spiritual grace', as a Victorian mystical poet put it.

And yet, when all is said, Christ is the crown of all knowledge, and 'the nature of all knowledge is best understood in the knowledge of the highest'. He makes sense of everything in creation below him, and stands as the window and gateway to what is above him. 'He that has seen me has seen the Father. No man has seen God at any time. The only-begotten Son, who is in the bosom of the Father, he has declared him.'

But lastly, this sense of the presence of God, the sight of God, the glory of God, is at its maximal not when gazing at sunsets or even at 'the glory of her hair', but in contemplative prayer, for which I take it the proper English equivalent is brooding or reverie, when every hint of mystery and marvel, but also the homeliness of God, is fused into one inexpressibly intense awareness, which is an actual foretaste of our final destiny and bliss, our last end and only good.

So you see, it means rigour: an hour a day at the least given to prayer. Your sole aim as Christians, the sole aim of religion and of all you do corporately and individually is to help you to embody this vision, in every act, private and public, moral, ecclesiastical, civic or political; to help you to see God, and to know what you mean when you pray Moses' prayer: 'I beseech thee, show me thy glory.'

John Byrom is a Canon Emeritus of Ely Cathedral and a spiritual director.

From Prison

CAROL

Nothing had gone right all day. I knew I had hurt my daughter very much during a visit a few days before and although I had said I was sorry I felt I hadn't done enough. I badly needed to find somewhere quiet to get my thoughts into some kind of order. That evening in my room I tried really hard to relax and say a prayer but the more I tried the more my mind returned to the noise around me. I sat on a chair beside my bed leaning against my pillow. Still the noise went on and on. I'd been searching all day for somewhere quiet and it really did seem that I wasn't going to get any. Then after about an hour of struggling to pray, everything went quiet and I fell asleep right in the middle of my prayers. While I slept I had the most amazing dream. It was so real that when I woke I just had to write it down.

Only a dream but so very, very real. I know it's three o'clock in the morning but I must get this on paper before I forget. Dreams often disappear, and this one I feel I must remember.

At first everything was calm. I was sitting on a rock, nobody was about. I was at the top of a mountain. It was just the place I'd been looking for. Somewhere I could be alone, somewhere to find peace so that I could talk to Jesus and ask him to forgive me. I'd made a mess of things once again. Suddenly dark clouds began to gather, the wind blew hard. Then it began to rain, cold stinging rain lashing at me. There was no shelter. I had nowhere to run. I thought at first that I would go down the hill where there might possibly be somewhere to shelter but then it thundered, a big almighty crash and then the lightning. I just couldn't move, I was too scared.

I fell to my knees and asked God to help me. As I lifted my head and opened my eyes I saw a light shining from a tiny window. I hadn't seen any building there before but I was too cold to worry about that, all I could think was at least there would be some shelter. I ran towards the light. Looking through the window I saw someone I was sure I knew. Then as the truth dawned on me I turned away. I couldn't knock on that door, I couldn't intrude, shelter or no shelter I had no right to be under the same roof as Jesus. I began to walk away but he heard me. Still I couldn't turn until I heard a voice so full of love say, 'Carol, come in out of the rain, can't you see the door is open?' I turned back and all that fear disappeared as he smiled just for me and beckoned me inside.

Then the door closed, just me and Jesus. Maybe the storm was still raging outside – I don't know. Inside it was so calm and so peaceful, nothing but a gentle crackling of the logs on the fire. I wasn't afraid but suddenly I felt I couldn't look at him again. I felt a hand touch my shoulder and guide me to the fire and then that voice again. 'Sit down and warm yourself, then we can talk. I know you've been looking for me.' Still I couldn't look at him but I sat on the floor in front of the fire and just kept my eyes to the floor. 'Look at me Carol'. Again that voice, so few words but telling me I had no need to fear. Then I lifted my head and looked into his eyes, then I dropped my gaze to the floor again. It was hard to look into eyes that searched the deepest corners of my heart, eyes that could see everything I had ever done right or wrong and also the very thing I had been asking him to forgive. Although it was hard to look at him it was harder not to look. So after a little while I looked again into those dark, clear, steady quiet eyes and found them not only searching but shining, not because my sins didn't matter but shining with compassion that went beyond what I had done and saw the desire I had to serve him.

In that moment in those wonderful eyes I saw all my dreams and the answer to all my prayers. I knew that he believed in me. I was gaining more and more confidence as I sat there looking at him. I can never have a faith like this, but I could feel my faith growing stronger and stronger. I knew I could face anything now. He said very little, but his presence said everything.

The storm had passed and it was time to go. It was late but I didn't care. He walked with me a little way. Then he turned back. I wanted to go back with him. The thought of parting seemed more than I could bear. Then I felt that I can never really be parted from him. Though he goes his way and I go mine. Something wonderful has happened. He is still with me. He hasn't gone back after all. He is right here inside me. It is as though my heart is that building and I have gained him for ever. There are no words to describe how I feel. I am not just me anymore. I am free, and I feel so full of joy that all I want is to show everyone my love for Jesus.

I walked back down the mountain, back to a life I know can never be the same again. Inside my heart is a strength I have never had and a peace that can push away the worst storm. They do not belong to this world and nothing can destroy them.

Just a dream maybe it was, but not the presence that is so real still here as I write.

Carol is glad for us to say that she came to Christ partly through Julian Meetings whilst serving a life sentence in prison. Subsequently confirmed in the Church of England, she and other prisoners belong to the Julian group which meets regularly in the prison.

A Prayer
VENETIA CARSE

Let me live beyond the limits of my Self,
still in the 'now', yet on the edge of time;
eye looking inward, forward, down and through,
seeing always God's radiance coloured
in the mist, rime, blackthorn, shine.

Let me live close to the borders of belief
where differing ways converge towards the One;
and mind, drawing insight from the wiser heart,
moves stumbling on towards the truth
where knowledge, love and all creation,
merge, ignite, surge . . . atone.

Let me live where Christ, my faith, begins,
where love, confronting fear, holds candle to the dark;
rejection, rape – bitterness and pain
by his most Holy Cross so forgivingly redeemed.
Should we be asked to travel some dark road,
bruised, disillusioned, life meaningless, it seems,
may openness to God's all-giving
grace guide our blind eyes . . . through.

And shall we see once more and sense the joy
in small and patient things; soft mist, sun warmth
and blackthorn bud; or glory in a cloud
of swallow's wings. Then let us cease to strive
beyond ourselves and live, content to be, aware
of God's compassion . . . and His Love, which sets us free,
with prayer and reverence prepared
to care for Earth's sad frailty.

The Anchorite Cell
A Meditation on the Writings of St Julian of Norwich
VENETIA CARSE

These loving walls enfold me close,
This timeless Sanctuary – this Holy Cell;
My gracious Lord speaks to my heart
'Be strong in faith – All is loved by God

And all manner of thing shall be well'.
Low ceilings curve, encompassing
this hallowed ground of Prayer and Peace,
The starlet arc of heaven clothes
our strife-torn Earth, redeemed through Grace;
And God, so prodigal of love,
upholds all things, on earth – above,
in infinite embrace.

I sit here, I quietly wait,
a cob-nut in my hand;
I ponder, I contemplate
the Wisdom of God's mind,
And how so small a fruit
should hold within itself
The mystery of Death – Rebirth,
dark winter sleep – awakening earth,
God's loving care for Great and Small
made whole and perfect in a fragile shell!

Now, as day draws to quiet close,
Earth's plenitude unfolding slow;
As solemn bells of Angelus toll
and leaves, borne on late autumn breeze,
Fall, crown and shield the earth below;
Know ye 'All manner of thing shall be well!'
Know too, in time of darkest pain
(When seemingly estranged from God,
our future bleak, to hope but vain),
That He, our Maker, Lover, Keeper,
Still would have us know 'in Him for ever
Lies our healing, our Hope and Joy Divine'.

Before her retirement Venetia Carse was a Social Worker. She has been a long-time
member of a Julian group and of the Teilhard Centre.

John Cassian:
Early Christian Teacher about Prayer
OWEN CHADWICK

John Cassian is very important in the history of Christian prayer, living as
he did at a time when Christian leaders first thought systematically about

the nature and practice of prayer. Between 300 and 400 AD, many people retired to the deserts of Egypt or Syria, or retreated into what we now call monasteries or nunneries, in order to practise a life dedicated to God which was likely to include several hours a day of solitude. Cassian was not himself an Egyptian, but went to Egypt to study with the great fathers of prayer in the desert there. Then he was forced into one exile after another and ended in Marseilles, where he set up a monastery and a nunnery and wrote books in the western language, Latin. This made him the first teacher about prayer – and about the monk's way of life – in the Christian history of the west. He died about 433 AD.

If we summarise his thought, it went thus: What is the big problem? You long to get away from the distractions of this world, so you retire to some hermitage, and hope God will be your all and that the world will be forgotten; and after a very short time you discover that the world is not forgotten at all, that you worry about the next meal, or are angry with some passer-by, or dream about sex, or endure tremendous strains in the psyche, which the desert fathers thought of as battles with the demons. So it is not enough just to get away from it all and hope that you can think of none but God.

Therefore this quest for a very pure prayer, where the mind is steadily directed towards God, is one not to be achieved in a moment, and never to be achieved all the time.

It is inseparable from moral discipline and moral growth and is best practised in a Christian community. No one should rush out into a flight from humanity until they are tried and tested at length – hence no young person ought ever to try to be a hermit. We will learn to pray the better as our characters are formed under God's hands; and therefore shall learn to pray the better within a community and not in flight from the community.

Prayer needs feeding with matter in the mind. It is no good thinking that you can go away among the hills and instantly lift up the mind to your Maker and keep it directed towards your Maker. The mind needs to be fed; and the best words on which to feed the mind are the words of the Bible; and within the Bible many of the evocative words are within the book of Psalms, which are themselves a book of prayer and praise. Cassian's favourite text for this purpose was 'O God make speed to save me, O Lord make haste to help me'; and we still use that verse at the beginning of our morning and evening prayers because Cassian loved it so much, and found it so powerful in evoking prayer.

When the soul has come along this way, it will begin to find not only that it does not need constant feeding, even from the Psalms or the Gospels, but that such words, even marvellous words, get in the way. Then the soul is rising up to what Cassian thinks of as contemplation. There you are truly face to face with your Maker. And the experience is so overwhelming that words, even the best, most holy words, fade away, and if they are remembered they are an intrusion. In such moments the soul has direct experience of God, as though a flame of fire was darting out from the divine, ready to kindle.

No one can have such experience all the time, at least not in this life. These are moments of divine grace. Quickly the soul will need again the Psalms or the Gospels, and the nourishing texts of poetry and prose which evoke its higher aspirations.

All this may sound lofty and beyond a lot of us. But Cassian is very down to earth. Never are we to forget that all this is useless, perhaps impossible, except in relation to the growth of character. Cassian, having shown us the heights, pulls us down again to the simplest things – like greed, lust, arrogance, and vanity. Here he has the most sensitive psychological insight. It is not an exaggeration to say that no moralist in the ancient world understood the nature of temptation, and the weakness of mankind, with more depth than Cassian.

He loved God himself, obviously. He was sensible, often very wise. And it was his work that helped to make the Benedictine ideal, and influenced the practice of all Western and some Eastern monasticism.

St Benedict made the rule that in his monasteries a work of Cassian should often be read, and Benedictine monks follow that rule to this day. Cassian wrote good, though rather decorated prose. But his works are only exciting to read in some poetic moments, because subjects like sin and temptation are by their very nature monotonous. There can be quite long passages, sometimes, which make for tedium. Yet no one can read him with care and attention without feeling that this man was of truly great stature among the early Christians.

Some people called Cassian a saint; but for various odd reasons he was never formally made a saint in an important calendar; and that is a happy reminder that calendars are only symbolic, and that other men and women, many others, would in the seeing eyes of God be fit to enter such a list of saints – sometimes more fit than a few of those whom the Church now remembers with gratitude. So Cassian's day is 29 February; a real saint's day, but arranged so that we can commemorate him only once in four years.

Owen Chadwick is a priest of the Church of England and was Regius Professor of Modern History at the University of Cambridge.

Working With God

BARBARA CHARIS csmv

Most of us find intercessory prayer difficult. I think this is partly because we are daunted by the enormity of the needs, as well as the long lists. But is it not also because we tend to think that it is we who have to do the praying, that it all depends on us? The sooner we get rid of that idea the better. We must replace it by the idea that God is inviting us to share in his creative work, that the initiative is his, not ours. Perhaps we should ask some preliminary questions. When we come to intercede what do we think we are doing? Are we asking God to change his mind? Are we trying to manipulate him, or bargain with him? What do we think happens to our prayers; how can they possibly affect any given situation?

Intercession is not primarily a prayer, it is an action. The word really means something like 'standing-between'. It is more than a recital of names and needs, it is a sacrificial work, an act of reconciliation, a 'standing-between' with Christ. It is not a technique for changing God's mind, or trying to get something we want. It is a means of releasing God's healing power through our willing co-operation. This is a very heavy task, and one which we cannot do in our own strength, nor can it be done alone. Even if only one person is actually praying, he or she is acting as a member of the Church, and not as themselves. Christ is the supreme Intercessor. What we do can only be done in and through Him, or rather, He will do His healing work through us. The would-be follower of Jesus has been firmly told that he must take up his cross daily and follow him. There is nothing very startling or exciting in our daily lives, yet they are to provide the very stuff of which our spiritual lives are to be made. Nevertheless our days are very exacting and we are seldom equal to the claims and responsibilities that crowd upon us.

When we seriously begin to follow Christ, our love for God will grow and develop and this will lead to a deeper experience or level of pain than we have known previously. We shall be brought into the orbit of Christ's suffering love, and thus we shall be enabled to enter more fully into the pain and anguish of other people. As we conform ourselves to His will we shall be able to share in His redemptive work.

Intercession is much wider and deeper than anything suggested by those first questions, which now sound rather shallow. As our relationship with God grows, it will follow the same pattern as any human friendship. The closer two people become, the greater the sensitivity and understanding between them will become. The closer we come to God, the more likely it is that we shall be able to discern His will.

If we allow ourselves to be open to the Holy Spirit, it will result in a widening of our horizons, an increase of real love for our neighbour, and a deeper understanding of their real needs. Our compassion and concern, our sympathy and empathy will grow in exact proportion to the increase of our love and adoration of God. The work of intercession is now seen as something directly connected with our own personal lives. Its value is going to depend not on what we say, but on what we are. It is in this sense that intercession is more than a recital of names and needs. It is our personal commitment to Christ which is the vital and essential factor in this work.

We cannot hope to become effective, living instruments of divine healing and reconciliation if we are half-hearted followers of Christ. We may be inadequate, but there is no place for half-hearted, part-time Christians. Healing at every level is the primary concern of intercessory prayer. When we pray for others we are trying to bring the whole person within the sphere of the healing love of Christ. If our love for someone is deep enough to transcend our own selfish needs for a moment, we may be able to approach the most sensitive areas of their personality without trespassing, and so become a channel through which the Holy Spirit can penetrate and heal the hidden wounds in their heart.

I believe also, that this principle holds good for any one for whom we pray, whether we know them or not, and if there is any truth in this, then it will hold good also for all the wider areas for which we must pray in our distracted world.

True, intercession never strives for its own ends, or demands results. It leaves everything to God. In its widest aspect intercession is a vast network of intercourse between God and ourselves at every level of existence. It is an experience of deep love and concern on our part, caught up and transfigured in the infinitely deeper love and compassion of God.

Intercession is something which we dare not ignore, nor should we undertake it lightly. It is concerned with the deep, hidden purposes of God, and the deep, hidden needs of the human soul.

Barbara Charis was a member of the Community of St Mary the Virgin, Wantage, and was Mother General there from 1966 to 1975. She died in 1991.

Walsingham:
A Place Where Nazareth is Felt

CHRISTOPHER COLVEN

Many thousands make their way to the north Norfolk village of Walsingham to visit the Shrine of Our Lady, just as pilgrims did in medieval times. Our age may be characterised as being 'indifferent' and 'secular' but people are open and desirous of an experience of God, and the time-honoured way of pilgrimage meets a new need.

Does this make Walsingham an English equivalent of Lourdes, with all the excitement and razzmatazz of a major pilgrim centre? In God's mercy, it does not.

There remains something quintessentially 'English' about the village and its devotional centres. In these few introductory words, I am not trying to paint a picture of what Walsingham has to offer, or what is entailed in a pilgrimage programme – what I do want to open up for you is the particular emphasis on which the Shrine is built.

Legend tells us that in 1061 the lady of the manor, a certain Richeldis de Faverches, had a vision in which the Mother of Jesus appeared to her. She was asked to build a simple house, a replica of the home at Nazareth where Mary and Joseph had cared for the Christ in his formative years. The intention was that the people of England should come to imbibe the atmosphere of Nazareth, and through reflection and meditation should experience a deepened understanding of the Christian truth of Incarnation – that the Child of Mary is in a unique way the Child of God too.

Modern psychology underlines for us the growing understanding of the early years as being definitive for mental, spiritual and physical maturity in adulthood. 'The child is father of the man', and, for the Christian, the thirty 'hidden years' of Jesus' life before his baptism in the Jordan are a rich source for contemplation and prayer.

Walsingham's vocation is now, as it was in medieval times, to provide a focus where Nazareth can be 'felt'. Our Eastern Orthodox brothers and sisters have a great love for icons: to them, an icon is not a dead representation; it has something of a sacramental quality and it contains, in some mysterious way, a part of that which it depicts. Since the restoration of the devotion on its present site in 1931, pilgrims have come to the Holy House – the simple room which is covered by the Shrine church – to ponder the events and influences of Jesus' upbringing. I believe, because of the love and prayer poured out on that spot, that it is becoming an ever more true icon of Nazareth. This means that today in the middle of Norfolk a Christian can *experience* – and that is a key word – the atmosphere of the original home of Mary and Joseph.

Walsingham is first and foremost a place where one is immersed in the mystery of the Incarnation. Because that part of our faith is only to be comprehended in stillness and quiet, despite the large numbers who visit us, these qualities are at the very heart of the Shrine. There is something timeless and unhurried about even the busiest part of the pilgrimage season. Many who find their way here have been searching for Christian faith in a troubled environment. The Holy House, with its basic values of security, love, compassion, human dignity and respect for others, strikes a powerful note.

Many of our pilgrims have clear mental and physical handicap. For them and others, the healing ministry does have a very special role – the sacrament of the sick, the laying on of hands, the sprinkling with water from the Shrine well, sacramental confession. Since 1922, at six o'clock each evening the rosary is prayed and accompanied by intercessions. This is our special apostolic work and there are hundreds of intercessions each day. They come in to us from all over the world: the majority of them are left by visitors, but many come by letter and phone, and a few by telegram.

Walsingham's vocation is to be 'England's Nazareth', its witness is to proclaim the Incarnation of Jesus Christ and its spirituality is therefore very much caught up into the love of the Mother for her Child and vice versa. Anglicans often fight shy of affection for Mary and this is a sad part of our tradition. For Walsingham rejoices in the simple truth that, as his Mother taught Jesus to pray in the humble surroundings of her own home, so she helps us to a better understanding of her Child today.

Christopher Colven is Master of the College of Guardians of the Anglican Shrine of Our Lady of Walsingham, and Vicar of St Stephen's, South Kensington, London.

Meditation is Like . . .

KATE COMPSTON

Sometimes, some gifted times, it is like
a great white bird that glides
on thermals, effortless, with every cell
and feather attuned
to the lifting wind and
still, no flapping of wings, just
an occasional shift of muscles
to go upward again, to touch
the sun's rays, the grace of warmth.

It is tempting to think that this
is the zenith of the soul's pilgrimage –
this joy and rising.
And yet
something, some voice, insists
that when I plummet in the storm,
stagger on drunken feet
on crazy outcrops,
surprised and ruffled, like
a grounded jackdaw,

clownlike and
ridiculous, unable to take off
let alone soar
on the shrieking winds,
this is
or well might prove
the growing time.

A Feminine Spirit for our Time

KATE COMPSTON

The picture of the Valley of Dry Bones described by Ezekiel (chapter 37) seems bleakly pertinent today, as the fabric of our fragile planet thins and tears into holes. The continued stockpiling of nuclear weapons, the growing gap between the rich and the poor of the earth, and the ecological threats to so many of our life-support systems, could easily cripple us with helplessness and despair.

And the bones could become a great deal drier . . . unless, as the seemingly crazy old prophet Ezekiel envisioned, a new spirit blows across our arid world, shaking us, till we rattle, out of our thraldom to one-up-on-thou materialism and our habit of dividing, splitting and confronting, rather than harmonizing, negotiating and reconciling. We need to have new dreams, aspirations and words inscribed on our hearts. I believe that Mother Julian – along with Hildegard of Bingen, Francis of Assisi, and others – can help to bring us to ourselves again, and redirect us to a creation-centred spirituality which 'trad' Christianity has long tried to subdue. I fancy this wind of change has begun to blow.

Ezekiel uses a Hebrew word for spirit/wind/breath that appears often in the Old Testament, not least in the Genesis creation story. It is *ruach* and is a feminine word. The spirit that broods over the chaos in the beginning, and the wind that comes from every quarter to fill and animate the dry bones of faithless Israel is a feminine spirit. And I believe this small unfeted fact is symbolically very important. It is the feminine spirit that can breathe a healing hope into our fragmented world. I do not, of course, mean that it is a woman who will save the day but that it is the Yin rather than the Yang, in both men and women, which is being beckoned into the open by the Spirit of God. The qualities traditionally described as feminine are those which need ventilation and can offer ventilation to today's world.

The new science emerging from the quantum theory is now acknowledging what mystics, poets – and many women – have always sensed anyway; that the evolution and day to day running of the universe has more to do with relationships and nurturing love, which is a traditionally feminine emphasis, than with objective cause and effect of the Aristotelian splitting into categories, which is a traditionally masculine emphasis. All things are interdependent and we cannot stand aloof from other life forms or life support systems. Mother Julian's reflections on that 'little thing the size of a hazel nut', and St Francis' Canticle of the Creatures, both point us to this awareness. God is in the very processes of the 'seamless robe' of creation – animating, healing, and nudging humankind towards a 'SHE' future: Sane (peaceful, actively non-violent), Human (just, sharing) and Ecologically sustainable.

What the *ruach* of God urges of us in these times is the feminine response of gentleness, reverence, stillness and listening, to counterbalance the virile self-assertion, the noisy thrusting towards dominance, with which we have previously threatened the rest of creation. Greek culture forced wedges between sacred and secular. Now we need to see all created things as bearing the signature and life of the Creator; we must again engage with, not detach ourselves from, the earth and all that dwells therein.

Again, the Spirit of God calls for a response of co-operation and trust to counterbalance the competitiveness, the wars and one-up-manship with which we have hitherto raped the earth and plundered the powerless. We need a new vision and a new language to set us on the path towards initiatives in peace making and acting justly. We must name the idols and challenge the myths that have convinced us we are 'naturally' aggressive, competitive and possessive. We must educate ourselves to see the ease with which we project our own darkness on to others. If we can befriend our own shadows, we will have no need of enemies to act as our scape-goats. This self-education is a major and radical task for the Church today.

What this task demands of us are the traditionally feminine qualities of feeling, imagination and playfulness. We must give these values at least the same dignity as we give to analytical thought, logic and fact-mongering. Stories and dreams, symbols and rites, poems and songs need to come into their own again. For these touch and inspire us in a way that mere information cannot possibly do. They will give us hope, and draw us out of our isolation into community.

Finally, the *ruach* of God beckons the privileged and the powerful towards responses of self-limitation, caring and sharing – to counterbalance the acquisitiveness and insistence on our 'earned rights', with which we have previously subdued the earth and its people. As God's stewards, we earn and own nothing. Nurturing and care-taking, traditionally women's business, is actually the business of us all. 'Living more simply that others might simply live' might have become a trite expression, but it is not yet a widespread practice. So we need new political priorities. For all of this is political. Prayer is political. Whenever we pray, 'Your Kingdom come on earth as it is in heaven', we are acknowledging that the earth has an integrity of its own. The Kingdom is not some 'other' realm of pie in the sky when we die. Furthermore, we are leaning into a future which will only be realized as we make and follow through conscious political choices about the ordering of this global village. Because we are imperfect, operating within tarnished institutions, our choices will always fall short of the values of the Kingdom. But I believe that God honours our good intentions.

There is a nice story about some native porters on an expedition in Africa, who were being made by their masters to hurry through the jungle. Suddenly they put down their loads and refused to take another step. When challenged and goaded, they said, 'We will go no further at present. We have come so far and so fast that now we must wait for our souls to catch up with us.'

That is a parable for us and our day. It is time to pause . . . time to lay down the baggage of the masculine, and let the neglected feminine aspects of our spirits catch up with us. Then we dare hope, with our risen Mother Christ, that the dry bones will live; and, with Mother Julian, that, 'All shall be well and all manner of things shall be well.'

Seeds of Hope

KATE COMPSTON

Take time to be,
to feel,
to listen to the water
air
and earth;
creation's treasure store.
They're wounded for the want
of being listened to;
they cry
and too few hear;
they slowly die
and too few mourn.

And yet
through those who give attention,
who stretch both hands
to touch, embrace and tend;
through those who marvel, reverence and kneel,
who cup the water,
feel the breath of heaven,
and hear the humming earth –
a healing comes
and there are seeds of hope.

There is tomorrow
germinating in today.

Be still.
Be loving.
Persevere.
Be true
to your connectedness.
Be you.

Take time to be,
to feel,
to listen to the stories
            dreams
        and thoughts
            of those who have no voice.
They're wounded for the want
of being listened to;
they cry
and too few hear;
they slowly die
and too few mourn.

And yet –
through these who give attention,
who stretch both hands
to touch, embrace and tend,
through these who labour, claim their dignity
and drink the cup of suffering,
who breathe the winds of change,
and earth their dreams in struggle –
healing comes
and there are seeds of hope.
There is tomorrow
germinating in today.

Be still.
Be just –
participating
in their truth.
In finding them,
you find yourself.

Kate Compston is a United Reformed Church Minister. She is committed to family, writing, counselling and promoting stillness through quiet days and retreats.

The Jesus Prayer

C. CONNOLLY

The use of this prayer is very dear to the Eastern Church. The first Christians discovered for themselves the tremendous power of the name of Jesus. Our Lord said: 'Until now you have not asked anything in my name.' 'God gave Him a name which is above all other names.' To merely say the name of Jesus is to make Him present. To misuse or use in vain the Holy Name has always been reprehensible. It always will be.

Down the ages the mention of Jesus has been a way to holiness. Through the Celtic monks, who received their way of life from the Fathers of the Libyan Desert, the devotion came to these islands. Any prayer or invocation centred around the name of Jesus was more or less termed the Jesus Prayer. 'Lord Jesus Christ, Son of God, have mercy on me a sinner.' 'Jesus Christ', 'Lord Jesus.' The oldest and most revered form is just 'Jesus'. This is the one we are talking about. The prayer can be pronounced or just thought. It is borderline between mental and vocal prayer, between 'pondering over' and contemplation. It is a way, a method for all seasons – in church, in one's room, in class, shop, or office, at work or play.

Before pronouncing the name of Jesus we should relax and recollect before calling deeply for help from the Holy Spirit. Without the Holy Spirit 'no one can say "Jesus is Lord" '. If we once master with heartfelt worship the name of Jesus, we only have to fasten on to it, cleave to it gently, slowly, and peacefully. The name once uttered, and felt as the apostles felt and experienced Jesus in their lifetime, in moments of divine insight, is sufficient.

The influence of the Holy Spirit extends itself into our deep prayer life. It is not a literal repetition that is meant, but a secret quiescent pondering of Jesus in our hearts. Song of Songs: 'I slumber, but my heart is awake.' For some the name of Jesus will be one of many events in the spiritual life. For others the Name of Jesus will be a habitual method. For those for whom the Holy Spirit will breathe the Name of Jesus, it will become the centre and heart of their whole interior life, around which the special method of the Jesus Prayer will revolve.

The best prayer for each of us is, of course, the prayer to which the Holy Spirit calls us – through the events and circumstances of the day. However, the Jesus Prayer helps us to simplify and unify our life. Many methods may have wearied us by complicating things, when in fact, all that is required is that 'at the Name of Jesus every knee should bow'.

The adoption of this simple method must not be seen as a short-cut to sanctity devoid of self-denial. The Name of Jesus acts as a filter, which excludes all thoughts, feelings, words, actions, which are not of the mind of Christ. We must never cease convincing ourselves that as Jesus increases in us, there must be a corresponding decrease of our selfish selves. The daily death of selfishness – cause of all our sins and failings – must go on. Once we have made our decision and said our 'Yes', we don't have to try very hard, as we have already invited the Holy Spirit into our lives for the purpose of dislodging selfishness.

The Name of Jesus is a means of transfiguration – seeing God through things and people. We can transfigure in an extraordinary way our whole world in Jesus Christ. The whole universe is not only the visible sign of invisible Godly beauty, but it expresses Christ as Lord, and silently says the Name of Jesus. Should we deny this, 'the very stones would cry out "Jesus is Lord" '. As God's creatures, endowed with reason and free will, as baptised Christians, we owe Christ that faith and love that makes us say: 'everything that breathes – all things praise the Lord.' For example, when we say *Jesus* as we contemplate a person, a rose, a tree, we reach Him in the depths of that person or living thing or flower. We transfigure too, the birds and animals. Did not Jesus say that not even a sparrow was forgotten by His Father and did He not live with the wild beasts? It is, of course, when we meet ourselves as God's human beings and with the Name of Jesus that we are united to Jesus in the depths of our hearts.

After His resurrection Jesus often appeared to His disciples in 'another form'. So, too, He continues to meet us in many ways, but particularly in the form of people (our neighbours). What about the crowds we meet daily in office, shop, school or street? Do we really meet them with the Name of Jesus on our lips and in our hearts? The Name of Jesus is really our name and their name. Better still if the Holy Spirit allows us to see Jesus imprisoned in the sinner, the criminal, the prostitute . . . We can then go through life with a new vision, and a new way of giving our heart. To the extent that we are made instruments of the charity of Christ, to that same extent we transform our world, and make our own of Jacob's words to his brother: 'Truly to see your face is like seeing the face of God.'

Creative Chaos

JEAN DALE

Recovering from an operation which came at the end of a protracted time of family trauma, sickness and bereavement, I found great healing and comfort sitting in the garden in the company of a little plaster Buddha. My husband had bought him from a garden centre whilst I was in hospital and placed him, like St Simon Stylites, on top of the stump of a cherry tree which had been chopped down. He sits not far from the kitchen window, blessing the house with his benign smile and serene composure. Day by day, I sat in his company, looking at him. With my body immobilised, my

emotions anaesthetised and my brain seemingly paralysed, sitting and looking was all I could manage. Prayer seemed an impossibility. Gradually, I
came to realise that the sitting and the looking *was* my prayer.

I was reminded of the story about the death of Lazarus, in St John's
Gospel. As Jesus approached the house of his dead friend, Martha – that
woman of great and active faith – came out to meet him with her friends
and neighbours. 'Master, if you had been here, my brother would not have
died.' We can imagine the concern, the tears, the upheaval consequent
upon the death of a loved one. But of the other sister, Mary, we are told
that 'she remained sitting in the house', an evocative phrase for those
familiar with Zen practice, and reminding us of the other occasion when
she 'remained sitting' at the feet of Jesus.

Faced with chaotic upheavals in our life and in society, we can take one
of three ways. We can resist and fight, sink into impotent despair or we
can 'go with the flow' and let it be, awaiting the outcome or 'floating' in
the words of the Jesuit writer, Thomas Green. Obviously, circumstances
alter cases, and sometimes we have to stand up and be counted to prevent
injustice, but often, if we can follow the third way, we find that something
new and wonderful and surprising can emerge. We are often told that our
Christian God is a 'God of surprises'. We are reminded of the 'sacrament
of the present moment'; that God is present in every circumstance of our
life. But faced with the chaos that so often erupts, it is difficult to realise
that God is actually *in* the chaos. It is one thing to know a fact in the
mind, but completely different to know it in the heart and enflesh it in
the concrete circumstances of living.

Science has been bringing a new dimension into all this. Quantum
physics and the new science of Chaos are opening up exciting insights
into the nature of reality, and showing it to be incredibly complex and
full of surprising possibilities. The cosmos is being perceived, not in the
mechanistic terms of classic Newtonian science, but more as a web of
relationships, and therefore unpredictable, open to the unexpected. The
quantum approach to science perceives everything as a manifestation of
creative energy – everything in the universe is alive! Life comes to us in
lumps of experience, so that flowing with experience is important.

In recent years, physicists, biologists and astronomers have created a
new way of understanding the growth of complexity in nature – the science
of chaos! In his book *Chaos* (Abacus, 1988), James Gleick says: 'Now that
science is looking, chaos seems to be everywhere.' The creativity of life
makes complexity essential and chaos an unavoidable part of the creative
process. With the development of a new branch of mathematics called
'fractals' (computer-generated images derived from simple equations), it is
becoming possible to measure chaotic systems, such as river turbulence
or very rugged coastlines, and find hidden patterns of beauty and order
embedded in the apparent chaos.

'What is happening is that advocates of many scientific disciplines are acknowledging that our universe – at all levels of life – has a strange and amazing propensity that comes to light in dealing with irregularities and chaotic behaviour. It is as if the chaos is the precondition for launching the entire system into a whole new way of being.' (O'Murchu, in his book *Our World in Transition*, published by Temple House Books).

So I come back to my little Buddha, sitting serenely on his pole, and blessing me with his gentle presence, as I stand at the kitchen sink. And to Mary, 'sitting in the house'. For in a universe so vibrantly alive with creative possibilities, who am I to interfere with the organic processes propelled by that Creative Energy which we call God, and know as Father, Son, and Holy Spirit? It is surely better to give myself over to the unfolding events, not just to accept, but to embrace and bless them. Like the psalmist I can only wonder at the majesty of God, and the infinite, creative possibilities inherent in the very fact of existence, as I picture the spirit of God moving over primal chaos to bring forth order and beauty.

The chaos of Calvary stands at the heart of the Christian experience – failure, shame, torture, death, the past in ruins, the future terrifyingly unpredictable. We think of Jesus, silent 'like a lamb to the slaughter, he uttered not a word', and of Mary and John, watching, waiting. Calvary – the silence of waiting, the disintegration of death – leading to the totally unexpected surprise of the Easter Garden, the strange and joyful encounters with the Risen Christ. Faced with the unfathomable immensity of this Creator God of surprises, our response can only be one of silent wonder, waiting and watching for the miracles of new life, new hope, new joy, at 'the still point of the turning world'.

Journey to Medjugorje

JEAN DALE

Bosnia, ravaged by a bloody civil war, torn by ancient hatreds, may seem an unlikely location for a place of pilgrimage, yet that was our destination as we climbed aboard the Croatian-Airlines' jet at Heathrow, bound for Zagreb. We arrived at Split at midnight and the drive along the beautiful Dalmatian coast was punctuated by several stops at armed check-points, where our documents were scrutinised by soldiers carrying rifles. It was an eerie experience to pass through towns remembered for their beauty and bustle and see not a soul, not a light.

We arrived at our destination at two-thirty in the morning to find our hosts waiting for us with a smile and a three course hot meal! This was the kind of hospitality two of us had experienced before, but it still left us speechless. Those dear people, giving of their time and substance in such generous abundance, epitomise the spirit of Medjugorje. For a pilgrimage to Medjugorje, is not a journey to a shrine; it is a journey to a valley and its people, their homes, their land, their mountains, their way of life. It is impossible to separate these elements.

Imagine a wide, sun-baked valley surrounded by rock-strewn mountains, with a few hamlets scattered along the shelter of the hills. The fertile soil produces crops of maize; white farmhouses shaded by cherry orchards stand amongst rows of vines. In the centre of the whole valley stands the church of St James. It is large, with two tall towers and in the years before the civil war, it was impossible to hold all the visitors at the evening Mass, and they would sit in silent reverence outside on benches, on the grass, with the Mass being relayed by loudspeaker.

As the number of visitors increased, gradually accommodation improved. Public toilets were built (to the great relief of all) and the villagers, who at the beginning used to welcome people into their homes, began to build extra bedrooms on their houses or to invest in purpose-built guest houses. But the welcome was the same; the open hand of friendship extended to brothers and sisters from other lands. What had happened to convert these formerly taciturn peasants full of tribal and family grudges into a model Christian community of love and welcome?

Since 24 June, 1981, six young people from Bijakovici, one of the hamlets, claim to have been visited by the Virgin Mary every day, at first on the hills and in the fields, and finally in the church. The apparitions continue, although only four of the visionaries now have a daily apparition. It is possible to be present at the time of the apparition and see the visionaries talking to an unseen presence, although their voices cannot be heard. Obviously the large crowds who gathered on the mountains in the early days were viewed with suspicion by the Communist authorities, and the children were arrested and questioned. The parish priest was imprisoned for nearly three years but is now pastor of a nearby parish. During our visit to him, a party of Muslim refugees arrived and were cared for by his Catholic parishioners.

The visionaries have been subjected to all kinds of tests to assess their psychological condition. They have been electronically monitored during their ecstasies and found to be normal healthy youngsters. That they remain staunch, good-humoured, patient, courteous and solidly hard-working peasants under this barrage of publicity is the greatest testimony to their integrity. The Church is unlikely to pronounce on the authenticity of Medjugorje while the visions continue, but the Pope is known to take a great interest and some of the visionaries have had audiences with him.

The messages speak of peace and call for a radical conversion of heart, for fasting, for prayer, for reconciliation. The villagers are a living example of this and fast every Wednesday and Friday. During our stay we could hear bursts of machine-gun fire from the nearby mountains, but in the village all was peace and I roamed just as freely through the fields and on the Hill of Apparition as in the days before the war. We met pilgrims from Belgium and America and spoke with a Monsignor from Zaire. Something about the place seemed to unite everyone as brothers and sisters. Two of us had experienced this before, in 1989, when we had arrived in a very assorted group and grew into one family.

The highlight of our stay at that time was a celebration of the Eucharist around the dining table that had been the focus of our laughter and fellowship. As we consecrated the wine we had enjoyed for our supper and the bread we would consume for breakfast, the Upper Room of the Gospels became a living reality. This sanctification of everyday life is what Medjugorje is all about. It is seen in the daily rhythm of the life of the villagers, centred on and flowing from the evening Mass and Rosary, attended by most of them every day. It is seen in the exchange of gifts, from rosaries and icons to food and shoes. It is a reality that has to be seen to be appreciated. Here the Gospel is lived in very truth.

Medjugorje is an oasis of peace in a desolate land. We heard prayers for the Chetniks – 'who are our brothers, children of the same Father'. We heard prayers for the Muslims and witnessed the joyful reunion of our host with his Muslim friends. If the messages of Medjugorje had been accepted and lived all over the former Yugoslavia, we would not now be witnessing this bloodbath and outpouring of hate. In Medjugorje six very ordinary young people came face to face with Love and Beauty, which has transformed them, their community and countless thousands all over the world. Whatever the final outcome, a pilgrimage to Medjugorje is a holistic experience of the beauty of the commonplace, of the ordinary people, of the power of love and reconciliation.

It is for me and for many, a pilgrimage to the heart of our Christian faith, to Nazareth.

At the Shrine of Julian of Norwich

JEAN DALE

My rather unexpected introduction to the Julian Shrine came as I opened the door above the steps that lead down to the Cell, and fell headlong over a figure prostrated in prayer! This rude intrusion seemed to make very little difference to the two or three other people praying there, nor indeed to the unfortunate recipient of my clumsy embrace. After a few seconds of whispered apologies and reassurances of well-being, the silence continued peacefully on its way, enfolding us all in its warmth and depth.

As I reflect on this happening, many visits later, it seems to me to point up the essence of the Julian Shrine – a continuous, all-enveloping silence that goes on imperturbably day and night, against a background of city noise and city smells that surround it and are always present, but not intrusive, an undergirding of silent prayer and presence and intercession for the life of the city and beyond. It could be likened to the drone of the bagpipes which sustains the various tunes played on the instrument.

The little church of St Julian, rebuilt since the Second World War, stands right in the heart of the red-light district of Norwich, next door to a factory and approached down a narrow alley. A gate at the east end of the church leads into a pleasant garden, green with grass and trees. Here is a pleasing oasis in an area which is an uneasy mix of post-war council flats and decaying medieval structures interspersed with more factories and car showrooms.

The Cell, built on the foundations of the original where Julian lived her hidden life at the heart of Love, is an unadorned room some 18 feet square, reached via a few steps at the side of the sanctuary. It has a plain stone altar, behind which hangs a large crucifix, and there is a window into the church, similar to that through which Julian would have been able to hear Mass and receive Communion, and another window high up in the opposite wall through which visitors may glimpse the trees in the garden beyond. A rough piece of stonework marks the level of the original cell. There are plain wooden benches against the wall, and a few prayer stools, otherwise the Cell is bare.

It is this very bareness, this one-pointedness of a room centred totally on the crucifix and the altar, which gives the Cell its attraction, and is redolent of the life Julian led here for so many years. There is nothing to divert the mind; no splendour, no artistry, no music, just the total concentration of empty space hallowed by long years of prayer centred on God's self-giving love. The bare stones, in their strength and simplicity, breathe the very spirit of prayer. It is almost tangible. Here is no cosy quietism. On the contrary, one realises the strength in contemplative prayer which sustains all creation. This is one of those 'thin' places, a sacramental space where Heaven and Earth meet, a place of Transfiguration. To be wrapped in its silence is like being wrapped in a blanket. 'We are enfolded in God' says Julian. 'And God is enfolded in us' – at the heart of all matter, all experience.

So as we leave the Cell, and hear the lorries rumble by down the road, and pass the waiting prostitutes, and return to the fumes of the car park in the bustling city centre, we realise that no matter who, no matter where, no matter what, God is there, at the heart of all creation, God-with-us, Emmanuel.

Praying the Rosary

JEAN DALE

First, a warning springing from a deeply-held conviction: it is all too easy for silent, contemplative prayer to become a thing of the head only. As the Fathers (and Mothers!) constantly warn, the mind must descend into the heart. In seeking detachment, which is necessary, our prayer can too easily become cold and introverted, our journey become inward and not inner, our prayer-life become selfish and comfortable. The inner journey is to prepare us for the outer journey, the vertical is joined to the horizontal and we, with Christ, are pinned at the centre, arms outstretched. We are called not to cold, sterile detachment, but to a passionate and prophetic engagement with the world, to love as Christ loved, to be spent as Christ was spent. The detachment from self, which is a fruit of true contemplation, is the necessary condition for the passionate involvement with other humans, with all of God's creation.

These lines are written as a reply to those who see the rosary as too sentimental an object, and view with suspicion the too frequent repetition of prayers for the help of another. Our Christian faith, founded so firmly on earthy Hebrew convictions, teaches that we are not spirit and material body – we are one being. The idea of oneness – unity, wholeness, salvation, health – is the deepest message of all mystics of all traditions. To that ancient and hallowed intuition of oneness the rosary belongs.

Perhaps that explains why so many people of various denominations who habitually pray the rosary, *feel* something special, something holy, about the string of beads as they take them out and run them through their fingers. Our whole body can enter into the prayer. Our eyes experience the wholeness of the circle of beads, their colour and shape; our fingers touch pieces of wood or stone, or glass, hallowed, each one, as a prayer; our mind enters into the experience of oneness with the saints in heaven; our hearts enter into oneness with those for whom we pray. For it is as a prayer of intercession and as a prayer for healing, that I have found the greatest use of the rosary.

There is a quality of peace, serenity, stillness and gentleness about the rosary which makes it eminently suitable for use in healing prayer. The mantra-like repetition calms the mind and stills the body; the fingers have something to cling to. In so many cases a tortured mind or body can only cling and the beads are healing to the touch. Frantic fingers gradually slacken and become calmer. The mind and the body, praying together, become one and move towards wholeness and healing. The ears listen to the healing words pronounced by the voice: 'Hail . . . blessed . . . Jesus . . . forgive . . . pray for us . . .' Repeated again and again, there is a positive resonance established in the unconscious.

Through these words, The Word, Dabhar, God's Creative Energy, is freed to bring order to chaos, healing and wholeness into broken lives. Again and again we pray for the coming of God's Kingdom, the words of blessing and glory return to us in that exchange of love, oneness, wholeness, that lies in the heart of the Trinity. Many times I have prayed a healing rosary with someone in great distress and seen turmoil gradually turn to peace, distress to tranquillity, tears of sorrow to tears of healing. When praying a healing rosary, it is advisable to have a large box of tissues handy – as God heals, the heart can melt quite literally! The old is dissolved before the new is brought to being.

Two examples stand out. A woman in severe nervous breakdown, after years of caring for an invalid husband, and convinced he was trying to poison her, would only allow us into her room after a careful search and sprinkling the house with holy water, against the demons she was sure he was conjuring up. We prayed with her a single chaplet of the rosary. This had a remarkably calming effect upon her. We promised to come back in a few days' time. She was much more in control of herself on our next visit and we prepared to pray a full rosary. As our prayer progressed, I could sense a new peace, a new openness growing in her. From time to time she paused, and shed a few tears, but the prayer went on, enfolding her in gentleness and security, repeating the words of blessing and kingdom, and the healing name of Jesus.

When I left two hours later, I knew her healing had begun. From that day she has never looked back and is now fully healed and in full-time employment. Moreover, her husband is experiencing deep healing and her family relationships have also been cleansed and healed. What do I mean by 'healing'? Oneness, unity, wholeness, acceptance, joining together what has been broken.

This was the kind of healing experienced by a friend with whom a healing rosary was shared. We had originally spoken of the need for her physical healing from a variety of allergies which had reduced her to despair. As we talked it became evident that the real need was much deeper. Family relationships were torn and bleeding: a much-loved son had joined a fundamentalist sect and cut himself off from the family; she herself was experiencing, from these depths, the guilt of being born a girl after the death at birth of two older brothers. In the quiet of my living room, on a sunny spring afternoon, we gently prayed a healing rosary together, with many pauses for both of us to dry our tears. This was her first experience of the rosary. Brought up in the Free Church, it had been quite foreign to her. Yet two hours later she rose to go, with shining eyes, saying: 'You know, something has happened and it's something good.'

How do you pray a healing rosary? It is, quite simply, an entering into the mystery of Jesus Christ, his birth, death and resurrection to new life. Each decade (set of beads) represents one of the mysteries of Christ: the joyful mysteries of his birth and childhood; the sorrowful mysteries of his passion and death; the glorious mysteries of his resurrection and ascension to glory. The person with whom one prays is encouraged to enter into these mysteries to 'put on Christ'. So, for instance, you announce the first joyful mystery – the Annunciation – and in prayer ask for the grace of this mystery. You could say 'Lord, thank you for the good news of Jenny here. Thank you for creating her, thank you for the angel that announced her to her mother, thank you for the womb in which she was formed.' And so on, as the Spirit gives utterance. The person is affirmed and helped to accept the gift of herself, or himself, in and through Christ.

So you proceed, appropriating for us, in our needs, the life, death and resurrection of our Lord Jesus Christ, who was like us in all but sin, who suffered, but in whom Abba reigned as King and Creator. In Jesus Christ we experience our own brokenness and accept it. In him we pray that God's Kingdom will come, God's will be done, not ours. In him we accept death, brokenness, nothingness. And in him, from that death, that nothingness, we rise to new life, new wholeness, new possibilities, healed, put together again, but in newness, through the power of the One who makes all things new. We are letting God be God in us and for us.

And we are not alone; we undertake our rosary journey in the midst of the communion of saints, strengthened and supported by their prayers and the prayers of Mary, that blessed woman who stands as a model of trust and contemplation. For it is the prayer of contemplation that under-girds our whole spiritual journey.

The rosary can help to open up our own depths in the silence of contemplation and it can be a powerful tool of compassionate help for others. It has as many variations as there are people to pray it, for each person's prayer is unique, the prayer of the Holy Spirit in each facet of God's glorious self-manifestation. I can only encourage you to try it, and let the Holy Spirit pray God's prayer in you, through you, for God's glory.

Jean Dale is a Roman Catholic lay woman, a mother and grandmother and a member of the Julian Meetings Advisory Group. Before retirement she was a teacher of modern languages, and is now involved in the spiritual formation of adults.

Compunction

ESTHER DE WAAL

I think it must be because I have a highly developed visual sense and because images always mean more for me than a more cerebral approach that I have taken great delight in discovering and re-appropriating the monastic concept known as compunction. The word itself carries all sorts of resonances. Its root is *punctio* and it means literally to touch, pierce, prick – so essentially it carries a sense of stinging, the sensation of being pierced, pricked, feeling sharp pain.

Recently it has come to be used in a rather narrow sense of guilt for sin, feeling sorrow for personal failure. But it is in fact fuller and richer than that brief description might suggest, since that could mean little more than being faced with a sense of guilt. For compunction is describing the experience of being touched or pierced by the awareness of my true state before God. In the light of that I am stung into action. I am aroused from my torpor and complacency, my readiness to drift along, and I am now determined to do better, not for any negative reason of guilt but through a positive response to the sense of the love of God flooding my life.

As I look at myself I cannot, of course, fail to see the sin, and to be aware of my shortcomings. But I do not allow myself to dwell on this with any obsessive regret or guilt; there is no endless reviewing of past faults. Compunction does not point me inwards in order to trap me into yet more self-analysis. It points me inwards since it is there that my failure lies, not outside myself, to any external authority, system, demand. For this is my having been false to my own deepest and truest self which is my own likeness to God in whose image I am created, as unique son or daughter. My feeling is one of extreme dissatisfaction with my lukewarm, compromising response to this out-pouring of love. It is in the face of this love which accepts, forgives, and frees, that I am stirred up, spurred, stung into taking action – all the words that spring to mind are positive ones which suggest action. I look at what I am and what I could be and it is the comparison between the two that triggers me into new resolves to do better.

I am only too aware of the danger of seeing sin in relation to myself rather than to God. When this happens I find that it is likely to lead me to inner conversation with myself in which I review the past, possibly dwelling on accusations against myself, even recriminations against God. This is dangerous because it does not bring me the energy which leads to change. Instead of this deadening monologue, compunction should lead me into conversation, with God. For the monk every day opens with the words of Psalm 95, 'Today – today if you will hear my voice, harden not your heart.' Monastic spirituality is spirituality of the heart, not of the will or the intellect, much less of any external programme or project promoted by the ecclesiastical structure. It is an invitation to enter into my own deepest centre from where I find God and from where I build my life of continual, unselfconscious prayer.

Seen in this context compunction is one of the components of the climate of prayer. It is linked with love, with reliance on grace, with trust in the mercy of God. Compunction cannot let me think of sin without yearning ever more strongly to respond to those ever-open arms of the Father who forgives us even before we have turned towards him. Like the prodigal, as soon as I actually hear and become aware of where I am and what has gone wrong, I turn and return. I take the action that will begin the journey home. My heart has been pierced as if by a dart of love and I can hardly fail to respond.

Esther de Waal is a writer and giver of retreats whose main interests are Benedictine and Celtic spirituality.

Thomas à Kempis
BILL DOWLING

Germany's great ascetical writer, Thomas à Kempis, was born Thomas Hennerken at Kempen, near Cologne, of poor parents in c. 1380. He was educated at Deventer in Holland in the school of the Brethren of the Common Life, and in 1400 entered the Augustinian house at Agnietenburg, near Zwolle, of which his older brother, John, was a co-founder. Here Thomas spent the rest of his life writing, preaching, copying manuscripts, and engaging in other scholarly pursuits. He was widely sought after as a spiritual adviser. His writings were many and varied, but all were pervaded with the choice devotional spirit of *The Imitation of Christ*. He said, 'Jesus hath now many lovers of His heavenly kingdom, but few bearers of His cross'. He himself was a devoted lover of the Holy Cross, and ever since *The Imitation of Christ* was first published in 1470, he has spoken to men and women across all our denominational boundaries, to both Catholic and Protestant.

John Wesley strongly disapproved of the fourteenth-century German mystic Johann Tauler, but he heartily approved of Thomas à Kempis. He even described him in a summary of *The Imitation*; 'As to his person, he was of low stature, of a ruddy but brown complexion, and a lively, piercing eye.' *The Imitation* was commended to all Wesley's Methodists. 'The style of this treatise is the most plain, simple, and unadorned, that can be conceived . . . A serious mind will never be sated with it, though it were read a thousand times over; for those general principles are as fruitful seeds of meditation, and the stores they contain can never be exhausted.'

Some of us have found this to be so, and Thomas has become a familiar friend; he is both charming and challenging. He wrote, 'A humble knowledge of thyself is a surer way to God than a deep search after learning.' He may have been a monk, but he appreciated the fellowship of others, 'Discourse of spiritual things doth greatly further our spiritual growth, especially when persons of one mind and spirit associate together in God.' If we should be short-tempered with others he reminds us, 'Endeavour to be patient in bearing with the defects and infirmities of others, of what sort soever they be: for that thyself also hast many failings which must be borne with by others.' He also bids us, 'Never be entirely idle; but either be reading, or writing, or praying, or meditating, or endeavouring something for the public good.' Thomas à Kempis also had acute psychological insight: 'Man looketh on the countenance, but God on the heart. Man considereth the deeds, but God weigheth the intentions.'

However, most readers of *The Imitation* treasure the passages where in devout simplicity Thomas à Kempis speaks of Christ and the 'inward life'. 'When Jesus is present, all is well, and nothing seems difficult; but when Jesus is not present, everything is hard . . . Most poor is he who liveth without Jesus; and he most rich who is dear to Jesus . . . Love all for Jesus, but Jesus for himself.' He goes on to say, 'Many follow Jesus unto the breaking of bread, but few to the drinking of the cup of his passion . . . But they who love Jesus for his own sake, and not for some special comfort which they receive, bless him in all tribulation and anguish of heart, as well as in the state of highest comfort.'

Thomas à Kempis lived in a monastery, of course, and there are obvious reflections of this in his meditations, but his wisdom has escaped over the wall to the benefit of all who over the centuries have read and pondered the simple but stringent words of his teaching. Many have prayed this modest little prayer; 'O God, who art truth, make me one with thee in everlasting love.'

If you do not know Thomas à Kempis, you will find him published in several editions, even in a paperback, (Penguin classics) and a few pounds spent on *The Imitation* will place a treasure on your bookshelf.

Bill Dowling is a Presbyterian minister with Methodist origins.

Two Haiku

ENA EDWARDS

> When least expected
> Perhaps an angel or two
> Whisper in your ear
>
> Sink into silence
> Let waves of it enfold you
> Be centred on God

Ena Edwards is a grandmother and a keen gardener. She discovered Haiku, a Japanese form of poetry, several years ago.

Be Still and Know

ALICE FAIRCLOUGH

In the silence are heard
Whisper, sibilance and sigh:
The breathing of the sleeping child
Cradled nearby:
The stir of mouse, insect and bird.
In the silence the Word.

In the stillness discern
The minutiae of form;
The shape and symmetry of fern,
The insphered calyx of the rose,
Delicate spearheads
Of catkin in repose.
In the stillness the Word.

In the silence far sounds draw near:
The cataract below the hill-top,
Laughter in the next valley,
The unseen lark we hear.

In the stillness the small
Encompasses the all:
The still pool accepts within its secrecy
The height, the depth, the mystery
Of the vast sky.

And in the stillness, I
May take the imprint of the Word:
In the silence, I
Receive the Lord.

Alice Fairclough taught English Literature in grammar schools all her professional life. She began writing poetry on retirement from teaching. She is an oblate of Stanbrook Abbey.

Introducing George Herbert

PAMELA FAWCETT

Elsewhere in this book Richard Harris speaks of poetry as 'a way of purifying and alerting the whole system for God'. This phrase is aptly applicable to the poetry of George Herbert, which is not merely a delight to the student of seventeenth-century literature but also a source of spiritual nourishment to the careful reader of today.

George Herbert was born in 1593 and died a mere forty years later. He was an aristocrat and a scholar and seemed to be destined for a glittering career at court, at Cambridge or in Parliament. It was not unusual for the younger son of a noble family to seek ordination and Herbert seems to have had a sense of vocation to the priesthood as early as 1616 when he took up the study of divinity. But it was not until 1630 that he was ordained priest and took up residence in Bemerton near Salisbury, his first and only parish. In the intervening years he served as Public Orator at Cambridge, and as a Member of Parliament, and moved in the circle into which he was born. There must have been much experience of tension during these years and perhaps the turning point was his marriage in 1629.

The Church of England in the years of the seventeenth century was indeed the 'Middle Way' between Catholicism and Protestantism, and had resisted the puritanical excesses that were to be a later influence. It was through this church that Herbert expressed his deepest devotion and faith and it is natural that he should use the physical structure of a church building as the framework for his book of poems *The Temple*.

The poems are not easy, being full of the startling images of the period and, of course, they are written in language akin to that of Shakespeare, that is sometimes strange to the modern reader. In spite of these difficulties, the depth of passionate faith and the integrity of the writer often shine through and are always there to be revealed by patient study. Herbert's was not an easy, sunshiney faith. It grew out of the tensions of struggle both intellectual and spiritual. The little poem 'Bitter Sweet' expresses this attitude which permeates many of the poems:

> Ah my dear angry Lord,
> Since thou dost love, yet strike;
> Cast down, yet help afford;
> Sure I will do the like.
> I will complain, yet praise;
> I will bewail, approve:
> And all my sour-sweet days
> I will lament, and love.

But also, there are poems where an untroubled faith shines out, coupled with a moving humility, as in the poem, 'Praise', (well-known as the hymn 'King of glory, King of peace.')

To gain an insight into the poems and the man who wrote them, it is worth while to turn to his prose work *The Country Parson*, published together with the poems and some very helpful introductory material in SPCK's *Classics of Western Spirituality* series. In it, Herbert outlines the duties, attitudes and lifestyle of a country parson in an age when this office embraced many duties that today would be taken over by the doctor, social worker or school teacher. As he describes this life lived for God and his people, his faith and utter integrity shine through.

If you visit Bemerton today you will not find much there to help you recapture those three brief years of ministry in the middle of the seventeenth century. The industrial life of Salisbury has crept over the water meadows, bringing town to what was once quiet countryside. Although there is a plaque in the little church, nothing marks the burial place of Herbert. But through the poems and in the pages of *The Country Parson* we can step into that so-different world and meet one of the most holy of English men.

The Rosary: An Historical Note

PAMELA FAWCETT

Did you know that until the fifteenth century, the word bead (or bede) meant a prayer? Owing to the use of rosaries, the word was transferred to the little objects with a hole through them that we now usually use for decoration. All the great religions have a tradition of strings of beads or knots for the counting of mantras. The usual number for Eastern religious is 108 – a 'perfect' number ($1 \times 2 \times 2 \times 3 \times 3 \times 3$).

The Eastern Orthodox used knotted wool 'ropes' to count the Jesus Prayer – either 33 knots (for the years of Jesus' earthly life) or 50 or 100. These are supposed to have been invented by St Anthony the Great in the third century.

St Bridget of Kildare, who died in 523, was buried with a string of beads and there is plenty of evidence to show that prayers (probably 'Our Father's') were counted in this way.

The word rosary means a rose-garden and was originally applied to written collections of devotions to Mary. The two concepts came together in the modern rosary of the Western Church. The 150 beads of the full rosary relate to the number of Psalms, which are also often divided into three sets of 50.

Legend attributes the inventions of the Western rosary to St Dominic, but there is no historical support for this. It was in the last quarter of the fifteenth century that the familiar shape and use became established. Today the rosary is used by many Christians and among the excellent books to help you pray this way are Robert Llewelyn's *A Doorway to Silence* and *Five for Sorrow, Ten for Joy*, by Methodist Minister J. Neville Ward (both DLT).

The Church of St Gervais, Paris

PAMELA FAWCETT

It was a different kind of pilgrimage that led us to this church in the heart of Paris. My son, James, is a musician and it was he who found his way to St Gervais, having discovered that this was the church at which Francois Couperin the Great was organist at the end of the seventeenth century. He soon discovered that this ancient gothic church was still a living witness to Christ in the twentieth century.

The Church of St Gervais lies behind the Hotel de Ville and is built on the site of a sixth-century church. The present building is of various periods; mainly of the thirteenth, fifteenth, and sixteenth centuries. There is some sixteenth-century glass and there are furnishing and tombs of the sixteenth and seventeenth centuries. But this traditional building has come to life again since 1975 when it became the centre of worship for the Fraternities of Jerusalem. These are two closely associated communities of monks and nuns who were invited by the Cardinal Archbishop of Paris to live and pray in the centre of this city.

My first visit there was on 14 July when the whole of Paris was given over to the celebration of the Storming of the Bastille and crowds and fireworks ruled. Inside the church was a cool silence and the visitors were praying as well as sight-seeing.

All the old seating has been removed from the church and the floor covered with carpet. There are some stools for sitting at the sides of the nave and prayer stools at the front and around – otherwise there is space for standing, prostration or kneeling. This has had the effect of transforming a rather overpowering, not very smart, city church into a space where prayer is as natural as the waters of a mountain stream.

The prayer times of the community are set to flow in with the life of the city. Workers can begin or end their day by joining in the corporate silences and offices or Eucharists of the brothers and sisters. At the Eucharist on Sunday, there is beautiful singing and music and people of all ages and nationalities are at home there.

The Rule of Life of the Jerusalem Communities was published in 1985 by DLT under the title *A City not Forsaken*.

Pamela Fawcett is an Anglican priest working in the Norwich Diocese where she is the Assistant Director for Ordinands and Consultant for Women's Ministry. She has been editor of *The Julian Meetings Magazine* since 1982 and is a member of the Advisory Group.

Reflections on Lourdes

How it began . . . JAMES FAWCETT
with thanks to Mme Leonie Tendron

Marie Bernarde ('Bernadette') Soubirous was born in 1844 at Lourdes, the eldest child of an impoverished miller. Fragile from birth, she was left permanently asthmatic by cholera at the age of eleven. On 11 February, 1858, when she was fourteen, she had the first of a series of eighteen visions which was to make Lourdes one of the great places of pilgrimage in Christendom.

Bernadette had stopped outside a cave on the bank of the River Gave to take off her shoes to cross a stream. She looked up towards the cave on hearing a sound.

'I saw a lady clothed in white. She had a white dress and a blue belt and a yellow rose on each foot, the colour of the chain of her rosary. When I had seen this I rubbed my eyes. I thought I was mistaken. I put my hand in my pocket. I found my rosary there.

'I wanted to make the sign of the cross, but I couldn't bring my hand to my forehead; it fell down. The vision made the sign of the cross. My hand trembled. I tried, and managed to cross myself. I said my rosary. The vision ran through her beads but her lips didn't move. When I finished my rosary the vision suddenly disappeared.'

When the vision spoke to Bernadette on the third occasion, she was instructed to tell the priests to build a chapel, to drink from a spring in the cave, and to return each day for fifteen days. Bernadette asked repeatedly who she was. She eventually replied 'I am the Immaculate Conception'. Bernadette described 'the lady' as appearing no older than herself, and they apparently talked and laughed together in the local dialect.

Some of the later visions took place in the presence of crowds of people, but no one claimed at the time to have seen or heard anything besides

Bernadette, who was ridiculed for some of her behaviour, at one point having been instructed to eat grass as a sign of penitence. A spate of false visionaries increased the scepticism of the Commission of Enquiry which had been set up to investigate the apparitions, but it was eventually won over by Bernadette's honesty and simplicity.

Bernadette died in 1879 aged 35 at the Convent of the Sisters of Charity at Nevers which she had resolved to enter thirteen years before. She was canonised in 1933, not only because of her visions, but also in recognition of her humility and the religious trustingness that characterised her life.

Pilgrims to Lourdes, then, honour not only Our Lady but also St Bernadette. They can visit her birthplace, the shepherd's cottage where she was nursed through infancy, and the cell where her family lived in poverty, as well as the cave and the basilicas and churches.

James Fawcett is the son of Llewelyn and Pamela Fawcett. He and his French wife are both violin makers working in Suffolk.

. . . and a pilgrim sees 'the Miracle'

JEAN DALE

'Would you like to come to Lourdes? I've been asked to chaperone some sixth-formers, and I'd like to have a companion.' My friend's invitation was quickly accepted – I am never one to refuse the offer of a trip to France! As this one drew nearer, however, I began to wonder just what I had let myself in for. A diocesan pilgrimage consisting of over 700 people, including 200 seriously ill in wheelchairs and hospital beds; a 24-hour journey by boat and train; ten days of noise and bustle and people and processions! I quickly snatched a few days of silence in a contemplative community, and hoped that would see 'this Julian' through the noisy days ahead.

Lourdes began to work its miracle on the dingy quayside at Newhaven harbour, lined with row after row of hospital beds and wheelchairs, each with its precious cargo of humanity. Some were less ill or crippled than others, some obviously fearful of the long journey ahead, but most of them seemed bright with expectation. There were scores of young helpers quietly attending to their needs, with smiles of welcome and friendship that were to remain constant throughout the pilgrimage.

These young people *pay* over £200 for the privilege of tending the sick pilgrims. The young men – 'brancardiers' – work like slaves to lift and carry the sick, in their beds and wheelchairs, enabling them to join the processions, attend the Masses, and take part in the Way of the Cross. The girls are known as 'handmaids', and are there to feed, clothe and wash the sick, even help them to the toilet. These are not trained nurses, just ordinary young folk who give of themselves to the full to help others, frequently strangers, and often they return home completely exhausted. There are, of course, trained doctors and nurses who travel with the pilgrimage and the helpers work under their guidance.

So the journey began, and as the days wore on, shared work and prayer, laughter and tears, food and drink, did their job of weaving one family out of so many strands. And in the midst of so much evident pain and suffering, my overwhelming memory is of song and dance and laughter.

What strange contrasts there are in Lourdes! Bustling streets, noisy crowds, heavy-busted Italian matrons with fearsome handbags, heavy-eyed children in wheelchairs, and souvenir shops lining every street. Then one reaches the Domain and, passing through the iron gates reminiscent of a municipal park, one enters an altogether different world. Our Lady's Domain, the 'real' Lourdes, contains the river, and on its banks the Grotto at which Bernadette received her visions, the large Basilica subsequently built on the hillside above the Grotto, the Baths with their famous Lourdes water, acres of open space, green meadows and flower beds, the Hospital for sick pilgrims, and, most impressive of all, the enormous new underground Basilica, as big as Wembley Stadium near London, yet only visible above ground as a rather elongated grassy mound. The atmosphere in the Domain is always peaceful, calm, unhurried. Hundreds of people mill around from dawn until midnight, when the gates are locked, yet the noise and bustle of the streets outside are strangely absent, and the only thing one can buy is a candle. All else is free.

My first impression of the Grotto itself was one of utter tranquillity. There is always a small crowd of people sitting or kneeling in silence before it. Mass is said there several times a day, but at other times we could walk right into the Grotto and see the place where the stream first appeared. The waters now supply the Baths a little further along, where pilgrims come to wash in the Lourdes water, which for many is the highlight of their visit.

For me personally there were several very special moments. There was the International Mass in the underground Basilica, with thousands of pilgrims from all over the world. There was the Torchlight Procession which, instead of joining in, I watched from high up outside the Basilica. A myriad little candles brought a blaze of light into the darkness of the night. There were the Stations of the Cross, up the steep, rocky hillside, seen in the company of two sick pilgrims in hospital beds carried by heaving, sweating, smiling lads in the 100 degree heat. There we gasped, at the shocking arc of the tortured figure being nailed to the cross on the brow of the hill by two life-size bronze Roman soldiers. There was the happy afternoon spent with a wheelchair pilgrim, going around the town for some souvenirs and a drink in a café. There was the Fun Night in the huge tent across the river, with hundreds of people singing and dancing, when some of the helpers took the wheelchairs 'dancing' around the arena, to the great delight of their occupants.

Best of all, though, there was the all-night vigil with two friends at the Grotto. We sat in silence, sharing hot drinks from the flask against the damp of the night air. From time to time people would arrive, to sit, to kneel, to pray. Helpers from the Hospital, on their way back to bed, would pause for a few minutes of silence. A young priest spoke gently with a weeping girl. Two women prayed softly with the distraught mother of a dying child. And at three in the morning, for a full half-hour, the most beautiful silence I have ever experienced, soft, warm, gentle, hovering like a dove.

The peace of that night is a gift I treasure. It is the spirit of Lourdes which underlies all the bustle and noise of people's lives, all the pain and discomfort of the sick, all the sweat and hard labour. Not all come away physically healed. We have the grime and drudgery of everyday life to return to, yet the healing presence of the Holy Spirit, the fountain of life, is there for all who seek it - creating, redeeming and uniting in Love. That is the real miracle of Lourdes.

Silence in Scripture

LLEWELYN FAWCETT

What an extraordinary thing it is that for so long the value and the quite vital importance of silence seems to have played no part in the devotional life of many devout and earnest Christians. This is particularly odd when one considers the constant emphasis on silence in Holy Scripture. Again and again in the Bible the fundamental importance of silence is underlined. It is in the silence that the voice of God is heard, and the will of God is made known.

Moses, contemplating the Burning Bush, hears God's Voice.

Elijah, in the wilderness, suffused with self-pity, discovers his next bit of work.

The Shepherds at Bethlehem, accustomed to the silence of the fields, heard the heavenly song; apparently no one else did.

The Blessed Apostle St Paul, after his great experience on the road to Damascus, didn't go round discussing it, but went off into retreat, into silence.

To St Peter, observing the hour of prayer, God reveals clearly that in His sight there is no such thing as a superior race.

All the great events connected with our redemption took place in silence . . .

The incarnation, our Lord's holy birth, took place in the silence of the night.

The start of His ministry, preceded by the period of withdrawal into the silence of the wilderness.

The great mysterious event of the transfiguration took place on the mountain top, the place of silence and stillness.

The critical hours before His Passion in the Garden of Gethsemane, in the silence, with His friends asleep.

The great stupendous happening of the resurrection took place in the silence of early dawn.

The prayer of silence is essential to any kind of deep relationship with God.

Llewelyn Fawcett was an Anglican parish priest whose ministry started in London and continued for many years in various parts of rural Suffolk and Norfolk. He died in 1992.

What is ME?

SALLY M. FOX

A Mother's Thoughts On Her Daughter's Illness

What is this dread, this curse, this thing that takes away youth and replaces it with continual fatigue? What is this sickness that changes young, strong legs that ran and swam and cycled into limbs that ache and waste away? What is this disease that takes a keen, intelligent brain and reduces it at times into a mind that doesn't even have the will to communicate simple requests or make basic decisions?

How can it be that Anna, a beautiful young girl can be changed into a tired, aching old woman who shuffles about in a dressing gown and nightie?

But new life is promised and resurrection will be ours one day. God has a gift as yet too precious to give. His gift is newness. Newness of body and mind. A strengthening of the soul. His gift is healing, restoration, re-creation. Part of this gift is kept for eternity, but bounteous gifts are here for us right now. God holds this gift of healing in his open hand; it is ours for the taking if we would but just understand that pain is for growing and darkness will become light.

God's plan for us is greater than we can ever imagine. Our being is so precious, our souls worth more than gold, and God will teach and test us until we are strong and ready. The gift is for the taking, but we just can't reach that far. So, little by little, God brings us closer and nearer to his great Fatherly love that will eventually give us perfection in the fantastic glory prepared for us by Christ himself. But we may have an element of that perfection now.

Prayer is never unanswered – it seems that the answer is, quite simply, 'wait'.

Sally M. Fox has two virtually grown-up daughters and is a Baptist Lay Preacher. She wrote her article in 1991, since when Anna has completed a university degree course, having made a complete recovery.

Silence

JOY FRENCH

Silence
Is more than a pause between noises,
More than the space between words;
Silence is herself,
The unknown queen.

Silence has power,
Which is why men fear her and seek to kill her
With chatter and clatter of tongues;
Man reaches for his drums, or switches on the radio,
Afraid of the voice of silence.

Silence endures;
When the drummers sleep, and the radio says Goodnight,
And even the dogs in the distance cease to bark,
Silence resumes her throne
(which was always hers; she has never abdicated,
merely gone into retreat).

Silence reigns;
And in silence, the self-deceived
Open their hearts to the truth
As they open their eyes to the stars.

Joy French was a retreat conductor before retiring to Devon, and was for many years connected with Julian Meetings.

Mysticism

EMRYS GEORGE

> Can I live with this word?
> I cannot live without it.
> Though I do not understand
> All mysteries and truths,
> There are those that I have heard,
> And know to act on gland
> And muscle.
> The tussle
> Of mind, body and soul,
> Naked in the presence
> Of loving divinity,
> Is real, and insupportable
> Unless transportable
> By sacrament and sign.
> Only the certainty
> Of the means of grace,
> And the hope of glory.
> Will strengthen me to face
> The Holy.
> The lowly
> Self abandons itself
> Successfully only
> In the open mystery
> That is Jesus Christ.

Emrys George is retired and writes occasionally.

Prayer and Poetry

RICHARD HARRIES

As a parish priest, I found that there were good practical reasons for reading poetry. There were few stretches of time when I could sit down uninterrupted to read a novel or theological tome. But there were plenty of snatches between telephone calls and rings on the door bell. These two-minute periods are so easy to waste. But with a little forethought they can be suffused with pleasure and insight by the reading of a poem. However busy a person is they can keep a book of poems by the telephone or in a handbag. But why poetry rather than any other form of literature? In 'Little

Gidding' (*The Four Quartets*, Faber and Faber, 1989) T. S. Eliot describes meeting a ghost-like poet from the past (perhaps Dante) and he writes that:

> . . . our concern was speech, and speech impelled us
> to purify the dialect of the tribe.

We are all subjected to a continuous barrage of advertising slogans, propaganda, half-truths, clichés and banalities. Unless we are very careful we will simply act as a drain for this verbal sewage. Recently, after I had led the intercessions at a Eucharist, someone came up and complained that I had prayed for 'Christians behind the iron curtain'. They were right to complain. I had simply repeated, unthinkingly, a propaganda cliché, thereby reinforcing in the minds of my hearers all their prejudices and stereotyped attitudes.

Poets do not simply repeat the clichés and half-truths of the time. They seek to feel more deeply, see more clearly, and think more honestly; and all the time to struggle for words with which to apprehend what it is that is taking hold of them. Poets are seers, seeing into the true nature of their time and perhaps into eternity as well; wrestling with their experience and with the words whereby that experience is both grasped and communicated. I have a notion (an over-romantic one, I know) that in a hundred years' time, when all our fashionable pundits are forgotten, some words on a scrap of paper - a few poems - will be discovered; lines written by someone living on the margins of our society yet so much more perceptive than the rest of us about what is happening.

Not all poetry has to wait a hundred years before its quality is recognised. But all true poetry helps to 'purify the dialect of the tribe'. If for most of the time we are simply pipes for the verbal waste of our society we can on occasions act as a recycling plant. But even so it is a closed system. We need the fresh springs of the poets to flow into us. Such poetry is more powerful than we allow. The Mandelstams found in Communist Russia that Osip's poetry, even when it was not on a political subject, was a threat to the system.

If such poetry is necessary in a nation permeated by propaganda it is equally necessary in a church cushioned by cliché, one of the great enemies of true religion. Ronald Blythe, the author, told me once that before getting down to his own writing he liked to read some poetry. It helped to prepare and alert his whole being. Monks have always read for a somewhat similar purpose. They have had their Lectio Divina both as a preparation for prayer and as a prayer itself.

Much poetry is suitable for this kind of spiritual reading. There are times for all of us when reading the Bible is terribly boring. This may be a sign that we need to be fed for a period by a different spring. Reading poetry can be a cleansing and inspiring alternative. But the same principle applies here as in all other spiritual reading. Read slowly, read little (one poem or less), mull over what is read, drink it deep within and rest quietly letting any simple prayerful aspirations towards God come if they come.

Most readers will know which poets they respond to and which ones they don't. Books of poems are still relatively inexpensive and it is easy to have a volume of George Herbert or Gerald Manley Hopkins or R. S. Thomas on hand. For those who are less familiar an anthology is a good starting point. Either the *Faber Book of Religious Poetry* edited by Helen Gardner or the *New Oxford Book of Christian Verse* edited by Donald Davie are suitable. The latter is interestingly different from the early collection by Lord David Cecil. For example, it contains quite a number of hymns. The inclusion of these makes a useful point. Many of our best hymns *are* poems and it is good sometimes to read them as such rather than to sing them. They, too, can be used for spiritual reading.

Poetry can also be useful in more directly contemplative prayer. Many people find that they pray most easily if they have a phrase or word which focusses the attention on God and which they can return to time and again when the mind wanders. The psalms, in some ways still our best religious poetry, are full of phrases which Christians have always used in this way. We wait upon God in silence and then say something like 'Truly My soul waiteth still upon thee O Lord' before returning again to the stillness, this rhythm being repeated a number of times. There are many words and phrases in Herbert or Hopkins or other Christian poets that can be used in a similar way. That great phrase of Hopkins for example, 'Mine, O thou Lord of life, send my roots rain'. Or, to keep to the familiar, the line from John Henry Newman's poem 'Lead, kindly Light, amid the encircling gloom, Lead thou me on'.

Some poems are really a prayer in themselves and Herbert is the obvious example. But many other poems contain words or phrases that can be turned into prayer. The golden rule, I think, is to turn these words into a direct address to God by prefacing them with 'Father' or 'Lord' or whatever we use. For however often we might repeat a prayer, using it as a scaffolding for the silence, we are concerned with a relationship, not self-conditioning. Repetition need not be vain repetition. It can be a way of deepening the relationship.

So poetry can be useful in two ways. It can be used for spiritual reading, as a way of purifying and alerting the whole being for God. And it can be used, as the psalms are used, to awake, express and carry our aspirations to God.

Richard Harries, Bishop of Oxford, is a well-known writer and broadcaster. His latest book is *Art and the Beauty of God* (Mowbrays, 1994).

Iona

MARY HOLLIDAY

'Behold Iona!
A blessing on each eye that seeth it.' *St Columba*

Iona is a holy place – a 'thin place' it is said –
Once the 'Druids' Island' now Christ's place of peace instead.
For 'Column' and 'Iona' are both 'dove' in symbol word
And Christian chanting came to be where dove and crow are heard –
Since on the Eve of Pentecost, five hundred, sixty, three,
Columba landed on a beach and built a monastery.
The monks mused on the 'white strand'; the hermit in his cell,
The 'North Wind' and 'Eternal Youth' are each a hidden well:
The 'Martyr's Bay' marks ancient kills, Kings rest beside 'death's street';
The spouting cave spits foam on high – lambs on the Machair bleat;
The 'Bay at the Back of the Island' is near the 'Fairies' Hill',
Its sparkling waves in evening sun are quiet but never still.
The Abbey and the Nunnery housed people versed in prayer
And holy healing herbs and stones still breathe the voice of care.
Today the tourists gather (but no crowds or noise can spoil
The yellow iris blazing firm, the patient, crumbling soil.)
And one was young and landed and walked up from the shore:
'Something about this place', she said; 'I've not been here before.'
Something about this place indeed – the pilgrims of today
Leave the Abbey's friendly cloisters and foot it to the Bay.
They sing and read at each marked spot, and tread the boggy grass,
The young and old, bright-eyed with truth, home in procession pass.
Here, 'Piskies' have the Bishop's House, the 'Presbies' have the Kirk –
A holy influence guards the land, lest ancient evils lurk,
Air's clarity lets being be, treads contemplation's measure,
In wordless stillness God is found – each pilgrim's holiest treasure.
The then and now are mingled here, and places hold their past –
And silence is built into stone, and stones were made to last.
The oldest rocks are these we hear – some fragments smooth
    with age
Translucent green, veined green and red, still writing history's page –
As swiftly apprehended through fine meditative mesh
God's presence folds attending minds in revelations fresh.
The Abbey lives, rebuilt in stones and lives of action rare:
The Nunnery may wake again to stillness and to prayer.
For prayer and action always meet where steadfast earth and sky
Help us to see the invisible, plain to the inner eye.

And much is seen in little things and time has little power:
Iona was, Iona lasts, Iona claims each hour.
Sun-sea-bird-bloom-rock-wave-wind-grass-myth-magic-holy
    peace –
In God all-wrapped, in Christ made clear –
Wait, listen. Here words cease.

'In Iona of my heart, Iona of my love,
Instead of monks' voices shall be lowing of cattle,
But 'ere the world come to an end
    Iona shall be as it was.'

Prophecy of St Columba

A Very Unremarkable Tree

MARY HOLLIDAY
Inspired by an 'awareness walk' during a Julian Meetings retreat.

Not a magnificent cedar,
Just a very unremarkable tree:
You are tall, you are varied in bark texture,
Immensely variegated –
Ivy clinging on one side,
Tiny insects in some holes,
Gummy outcrops –
Smooth parts –
You are even the tolerant end of a barbed wire fence –
Its knots are embedded in your uncomplaining surface.

You are very strong, though sparse in leaves,
Knotted and gnarled, with green moss at base,
Productive in dull brown needles, but not in cones:
Almost overwhelmed by other trees,
Yet reaching to the sky in a tracery of infinite delicacy.
Far above that strong indestructible trunk,
Holly grows protectively, the opposite side from the ivy –
Are these always to be symbols, however curiously,
Of divine incarnation?
    Are you me?
    Are you the Church?
    Are you perhaps Christ?
Or, more deeply involved in the whole order of things –
For as I place my three varied feathers –

Stubby black, long black and white and small white and fluffy
Against your alien texture
The Trinity, no less, has married another fragment of Creation.

Mary Holliday is a retired Methodist minister. For many years she was in the Farncombe Ecumenical Community of Prayer and Work for Unity. She has been much involved in the conducting of retreats, ecumenism and spiritual studies. She is a past member of the original Julian Meetings Advisory Group.

Peace Spirituality

GERARD W. HUGHES sj

When asked 'What do you do?' and I answer 'I work on the spirituality of justice and peace', I usually meet with polite incomprehension, 'How interesting. Haven't we had a dreadful summer.' So here, I offer one description of what is meant by 'peace spirituality'.

Spirituality is a difficult word to define clearly. It includes in its meaning the inner quality of our lives, the state of inner harmony/disharmony of our minds and hearts, of our fears and anxieties, hopes and desires, loves and hates, which arise through our experience of life and our reactions to those experiences. Spirituality is a shorthand word for the complexity of our inner lives, our memories, our mind, understanding, will, emotions, and it is out of all this complexity that our actions proceed. Spirituality is about the roots of our being. In Christian understanding, when we talk of 'the spiritual life', we mean the harmony/disharmony of all those elements of our inner life and how they relate to each other, to the world and to God, who is 'nearer to us than we are to ourselves', who is both within and beyond all things, the ground and granite of our being.

Peace spirituality means finding that harmony with God, with creation and within ourselves by focussing our attention on the question of peace. We do not have to focus for long before it becomes clear to us that we cannot build peace without justice any more than we can build a house without foundations. So it is more accurate to speak of justice and peace spirituality. It is wrong to preach peace and reconciliation to the victims of exploitation while doing nothing about the exploitation. It is even worse to preach peace and reconciliation to the victims of exploitation while at the same time living comfortably off the profits from injustice. As Tolstoy said: 'I sit on a man's back, choking him, and yet assure myself and others that I am very sorry for him and wish to ease his lot by any means possible, except getting off his back.'

One of the reasons why I asked to work on spirituality with people active in peace and justice, irrespective of their religion or Christian denomination, was because I had noticed the effect of active involvement in justice and peace work on spiritual growth. Such people tended to be more in touch with themselves and with God than those who were not so involved. Many of them began on justice/peace work without any conscious religious motivation and many had given up regular churchgoing and even prayer. But if they were at all reflective, their active involvement led them to ask questions which they had never before considered.

For example, they found that many of their friends did not share their concern and disapproved of their peace activities. The father of one young man refused to have the lad's name mentioned in the home for several months because the son had taken part in a CND rally! Those who engage in active justice and peace work inevitably meet with opposition, even from their own friends and family, and the intensity of the opposition and the violence of it puzzles them and seems quite out of proportion to anything they are doing. This is very hard to take and many a peace worker discovers that after years of hard work they seem to have achieved nothing except to lose friends, discover new enemies and lose any inner peace they may ever have had. Meanwhile, the arms race continues apace, the First World grows richer and the Third World poorer.

Some people, in face of such opposition from without and within fall into a state of nuclear depression, which immobilises them. But even they in their depression realise that they cannot forget justice and peace issues and live at peace with themselves, for they have been seized by something greater than they are – they are encountering God *tremendum et fascinans*, who both frightens and attracts. They are led back to the bible and begin to read it with new eyes, discovering that God is the God of justice, who liberates the poor and oppressed, who abhors every form of religious worship which is not the expression of a just, compassionate and tender heart. In their own helplessness and powerlessness they recognise Jesus and discover he is with them in their hunger and thirst for justice and realise that in spite of all the pain and apparent hopelessness of the struggle they do not want to abandon it.

So they experience a new kind of peace, not the absence of conflict, but a sense of peace within the conflict and a knowledge that God sustains them in their powerlessness and helplessness and that he is strong in their weakness. They begin to realise, too, that the hardest part of the struggle for justice and peace is the struggle against their own injustice and peacelessness, revealed to them in their reactions to the opposition they meet with. They cease to have illusions about themselves, realise they are no better than anyone else, become more understanding, more gentle and tolerant.

In our churches in Britain, justice and peace issues are muffled, labelled political, and so the faithful are simply left in 'peace', content with vague aspirations for the coming of the kingdom. We go on sitting on men's backs, choking them, yet assuring ourselves that we are very sorry for them and wishing to ease their lot by any means possible, except getting off their backs. What kind of God are we worshipping? If a preacher remains silent on issues of peace and justice there is 'peace' in the congregation. But consider what his silence is actually saying:

> 'My dear people, as a nation it is all right that our arms dealers should supply good quality arms to Third World countries so that repressive regimes may continue to oppress the poor and starving and that British dealers should make more in profit from these countries than government grants in aid. It is also right that the majority of our scientists should be employed in devising more destructive weaponry and that we should all contribute to the present and future armaments of our country, that we may afford to buy four Trident submarines, first strike weapons, any one of which has many times more firepower than the total firepower expended in the Second World War. This enables us to live according to the standards to which we are accustomed and even to do better. Let us thank God for all these blessings and be at peace, avoiding political wrangles about those who starve at our expense.'

Peace spirituality is necessary for salvation.

Gerard W. Hughes SJ, author of *God of Surprises* (DLT, 1985) and other books, is widely acclaimed as a writer, counsellor and retreat conductor. He is much involved in justice and peace work.

Love

GRACE HURRELL

> Awaking from sleep I found within me
>   activity of the spirit of knowledge.
> There was the vastness of God
> There was the multitudinous creation –
>   and He aware of every iota
>   He responding to every movement –
> Love: continual uninterrupted Love.
> Creatures, loving Him knowingly, or unknowingly,
>   in each reflection caught –
>   Striving to reflect – to imitate –
>   Love penetrates, enfolds, delights.
> The creature strives towards love,
>   loving the reflection, acting out all human-wise,
>   the action of love.
>   O vastness of the One Who Is!
> Inexhaustible energy in stillness –

> Inexhaustible care not overwhelming –
> Perpetually available
> Continually responsive
>   to each one of the millions of millions –
> With no diminution
>   no exhaustion
>   no withdrawal
>   no intrusion.
> What fortune to perceive the Truth
> to distinguish Being Eternal –
> then to love every reflection
>   yet remain open
>   to the penetration of the One.

On June 23 1994, Grace Hurrell, in her 98th year, entered into the glory anticipated in her striking poem. In her early days she was an open air speaker for the Catholic Evidence Guild and wrote books for children. She was instrumental in setting up the Chichester Julian Meetings in 1973.

Prayer Never Fails

MARTIN ISRAEL

To many of us, prayer is our private conversation with God, during which we tell Him of our needs and ask Him for help. Prayer is certainly the communion of the soul with God, in Whom we find the ultimate fellowship. It is also the ascent of the mind to God, in Whom we encounter the ultimate illumination. When prayer is at its highest, we are lifted up to a height of aspiration and performance that far outdistances our normal response and activity.

I believe that prayer works through God infusing His Spirit into the depths of the personality when we have left self behind and have followed Christ into the secret room of the soul. In that hallowed place we can hear, listen to, and obey the voice of the Holy Spirit, then place ourselves in faith and abandon to receive the power of that Spirit. It is not so much God answering our prayers by fulfilling our requests, as His making us more capable of coping with life by marshalling our inner resources and therefore being able to play our part as mature people.

In the Bible readings for the ninth Sunday after Pentecost in *The Alternative Service Book 1980* (1 Samuel 7:37-50) we have as the Old Testament lesson the story of David and Goliath It's a story that brings us back to our childhood. We have the stupid giant Goliath threatening the terrified Israelites to come out and do combat with him. They cower behind their miserable fortress, until the youth David comes out to meet the giant. He disports no outer strength at all, but has a lively mind. With his sling and a stone he stuns and kills the well-armed giant. But first of all he calls on the name of the God of Israel. This God filled him with fortitude and intelligence so that he could use his mind in acute reflection. Had he been in a state of emotional turmoil, like the Israelite army, he would have been equally impotent.

Whenever we see clearly how to deal with a situation that had previously eluded our grasp, it is the Holy Spirit infusing us with his integrating strength when we are silent and ready to receive his guidance. I believe this is the mechanism of all effective inspiration, even if we do not call directly on the name of God.

The Gospel lesson for that same day concerns Jesus effectively exorcising a child rendered epileptic by a powerfully evil spirit, even when His disciples had failed to dislodge the entity. He tells them later that this type of spirit can be dealt with only by prayer (Mark 9:14–29). Other traditions add the word 'fasting' to His reply. The disciples had acquired a measure of the Holy Spirit through Jesus' bestowing it on them by His contact with them. They were therefore able to do a certain amount of healing work and deliverance. However, their spiritual life was still rudimentary; they were to come to a far greater maturity after their Master's passion and resurrection, so that eventually they would be able to receive the full downpouring of the Holy Spirit from on high. At any rate, in relation to this clearance of the epileptic child, Jesus' supreme power of prayer was able to marshall the full impact of the Holy Spirit and expel the offending entity.

God acting through His Son can perform any sort of miracle. Jesus said that He of Himself could do nothing, but that it was the Father who worked the signs through Him. He also promised the disciples that they would do even greater works than He had, when the Holy Spirit descended fully on them. Therefore God acting in collaboration with prayerful, obedient, selfless humans can perform things that transcend all reason, because in this state the human assumes the power of Christ and does the work of God, the work, I believe, we were meant to do in this world.

But often our prayers do not work. We all know of not a few instances of promising people, often young and strong in the Faith, who do not get a healing from some progressive disease, so that they lose a vital faculty or die long before the usual span of mankind. In these cases there may have been massive prayer support, and the person may have been punctilious both in their prayer life and their general spiritual duties (these, of course, include our work in the world no less than our time in the ambience of the Church). These instances challenge our traditional faith badly, but, if they are followed through with clear honesty, may throw a new light on our work in the world and in eternity.

When all is going well with us, we are very powerful in the work we are doing, very sure of our own rectitude, and often rather censorious of those who do not measure up to our own high standards. We begin to commit the fatal sin of judging others according to our own high level of efficiency. And charity flies out of the window. When we begin to fail and prayer does not work the miracle we expected, we have time to think; just as Job did as he sat on an ash-heap, covered with a repulsive skin eruption. God did not remove his terrible physical, emotional and spiritual distress any more than He did St Paul's thorn in the flesh or His own Son's agony in the garden of Gethsemane.

But Paul was told that God's grace was sufficient for him, and that God's strength is made perfect in weakness. Prayer often works most perfectly when we have nothing to look forward to and only great regrets concerning the past. It is then that we can see our life in proper perspective and begin to realise how important our defects and sources of impotence have been. Had these been rectified or cured, and we were enabled to live what is called a normal life once more, we would have slipped back into the comfortable illusions of material security, popular emotional appeal and smug religious assurance. Being deprived of these pleasant props (and complacent religion is the subtlest of them all), we are forced to enter fearsome tracts of the unknown and mix with people and ideas that we previously would have shunned. As a result, a new way of life opens for us, and many talents that would otherwise have lain dormant emerge and approach actualisation.

Of course, if the person is soon to die, it is hardly likely that gifts will be manifested in what short span of life remains. But all is not lost. How we deal with the immediate period up to our death and how our loved ones cope with our imminent dissolution are also important matters relating to the later history of the personality in the life beyond death. Our stay here is a mere parenthesis in eternity, and we are building a spiritual body as we do our daily work with efficiency, honesty and love. Even when prayer seems to have the contrary effect of speeding on the very situation we feared most, it is assuring us that God is never far from us. Indeed, His rod and staff strengthen us even when we traverse the valley of death itself.

Prayer never fails, as Jesus confidently asserts. He tells us to knock and the door will be opened, ask and the answer arrives, seek in order to find. Our own dearest anticipations as to what the answer may be or what we may find in our searches may be ludicrously disappointed. But when we come to our senses we will see that God does know best, and that this particular circumstance is what is best ultimately for our spiritual growth. This is the meaning of acceptance, the true fruit of all heartfelt prayer. I can do no better than quote Reinhold Neibuhr's celebrated prayer as a conclusion:

Grant me the serenity to accept the things I cannot change, the courage to change the things I can, and the wisdom to know the difference.

Dr Martin Israel is a well-known retreat conductor, spiritual director and writer of books on spirituality. He is priest-in-charge of Holy Trinity and All Saints, South Kensington, London. His latest book is *Life Eternal* (SPCK, 1993).

Prayer in the Dark

MARGARET JARMAN

I keep seeing myself quoted in the most unlikely places, for instance in local church magazines of various denominations and from different places around the country. There must be a system for circulating useful quotes which will fill the odd gaps in church magazines and someone somewhere has fed me into the system.

The sentence they have alighted on is, 'I don't say I have found great light but because God is in the darkness we need not be afraid of it.' It is from a *Baptist Times* article in which I was interviewed about how retreats help me to cope with illness, but evidently it strikes a chord with many people.

All is not sweetness and light in the life of prayer, but contemplative prayer, such as is at the heart of Julian Meetings, helps us to trust in the darkness. The darkness tests our desire as to whether it is really for God or only for the experience. It teaches us that the awareness of the presence of God is his gift, not something we can turn on when we want to. But more than that, the darkness is also a way God uses to hollow us out so that there is more room for himself. There are treasures of faith to be found by trusting in the darkness which we might never have discovered if we had only prayed in the light.

Contemplative prayer leads us on to explore the journey beyond the clear outlines of day; beyond the precise definitions, whether of evangelical doctrine or the Thirty Nine Articles or whatever; beyond the felt experience of God's presence. Not that sound belief or felt experience are not desirable. They are important parts of the Christian journey. But we learn to go on trusting when God is more than our minds and hearts can grasp.

There is a good deal about this in the writings of the sixteenth-century Spanish mystic, St John of the Cross, particularly *The Dark Night of the Soul* (Hodder & Stoughton, 1988). In the darkness God purifies our jaded spiritual palates and burns away some of the dross that spoils our love. It is hard to stand before God unprotected by our own ideas and carrying no worthy achievements. But is not this what faith is all about?

Some people from my own evangelical tradition find it quite hard to understand that I am helped by someone like St John of the Cross. Yet his teaching enriches my own spiritual roots. But it is there in the Reformation stream too. A small book of daily readings with Martin Luther is aptly summed up by its title *The Darkness of Faith*. Luther emphasizes that we need to let go of our own plans, to lay aside all efforts to justify ourselves by our own work, and to try to be ourselves in the darkness of faith.

'Give me a light that I may tread safely into the unknown', we quote. But the man at the gate of the year says, 'Go out into the darkness and put your hand into the Hand of God. That shall be to you better than light and safer than a known way.'

The Revd Margaret Jarman was founder of the Baptist Union Retreat Group. She was President of the Baptist Union in 1987–88 but has had to discontinue active ministry owing to ME.

Into the Desert

MARTYN JARRETT

Desert places appear a great deal in the Bible. The experience of being in the desert is a profound part of the way in which we Christian people have talked about our relationship with God. A retreat in a beautiful place may not, at first glance, seem like the desert, but the symbol still holds good. We draw away from our everyday activities. Paradoxically, we then see more acutely what our everyday lives are truly about.

In the desert, all that was has now come to nothing. Whatever once flourished in the desert place has now come to nought. All has turned to sandy dust. As we are reminded on Ash Wednesday, 'Remember you are dust. To dust you will return.' In the desert, then, we see ourselves in proportion. Nothing is eternal; nothing, that is, except the immortal, the eternal, the unchanging Lord God himself. Nothing more brings home to us the reality of what it is to be that part of creation which we human beings are, than the theme of the desert. It is not without significance that when humankind has done its seemingly most clever thing and unleashed nuclear energy into our world, the image of what we have left is as old as that we were given in the early days of the Bible. We are left talking about a nuclear desert. The desert is a place that allows no distractions. The landscape is very much the same.

Into the desert Jesus went. Into the desert we go in retreat. The entry into the desert for us is not a physical thing. Nevertheless, it can still challenge. We are called to a different kind of desert, yet in it the same things are highlighted for us as were for Jesus. We are called apart to enter a desert inside ourselves, a lonely reality. Some of us try to keep that lonely reality at bay by never talking about our true selves, our true feelings, our understanding of the real meaning of life and of the demands it makes upon us. Sometimes it is as if we hope that somehow the toughness and hurts of life will never come near us. Don't talk of pain or separation or sickness or failure or death and, somehow, all these things will pass us by.

Religious people, such as we are, can play these games just as much as anyone else. We busy ourselves in the activities of the Church in order to keep the real questions at arms' length. We use the many activities and emotional uplifts that our churches offer us in order to keep the true issues of life at bay, rather than in order to look them in the face. Over-busyness is a renowned charm for achieving such an end. Even our prayers can sometimes be said as a series of reassuring charms rather than as a conversation with the living God who then might tell us things we find hard to hear, yet alone accept.

Deep inside each of us is a lonely space. Often, when we reach it, we find it more terrifying than any real desert. For there we meet our true emptiness. There is where we seem to find that all the certainties to which we cling might not be certainties after all. There we risk a desperate loneliness and meaninglessness about which we do not like to think. Unless we tread into that desert inside ourselves, come to terms with it, then just below the surface each of us is always going to be terribly vulnerable. A retreat provides us with an opportunity to go more deeply into our inward deserts. That is the start of making those deserts our friends.

Into the desert Jesus went. We are told that he was tempted by the Devil. Into our deserts we go. There is no escaping the fact that there, like Jesus, we, too, are going to be tempted. Charles de Foucauld, that great desert contemplative of our own century, has suggested that this is one reason why Jesus went into the desert for us. It was so that we might learn to expect temptation. Like the Lord, we might have to face that horrible temptation of taking short cuts and running away from those painful experiences which ultimately confront us with ourselves. Instead, as in the Biblical temptation narrative, we might make things easier for ourselves, make ourselves impressive in terms of this world, seek after power and influence. Christians in every age have opted for these things. Jesus was invited to make such a compromise. He withstood that temptation. We who belong to him are promised that we, too, can withstand if only we trust in him who is in the desert with us. We can feel too afraid of what we might be tempted to do if we dared to look into our deeper selves. So often we Christians can become some kind of Peter Pan characters, reluctant to grow any further into the stature of Christ because of the challenges it might present to us.

An acquaintance of mine delights to describe the favourite cartoon story of his childhood. An over careful man is leaving his office. He walks home because he fears the bus might crash. He makes a long detour because he fears he might be run over. He walks around a ladder for fear a bucket might fall on his head. He looks in a cake shop window and shuns all the goodies on offer because they might damage his health. Safe at home, he goes straight to bed to conserve his energy. And the last picture in the strip cartoon shows the ceiling falling on him while he is asleep and he is killed. We are often like that man, avoiding so much risk for fear we cannot cope. Remember, even in the perfect paradise, we are warned, there was temptation. Our innocence is not going to be preserved by opting for spiritual laziness which is, after all, giving in to temptation before we start.

If we do dare to go into the desert as Jesus goes into the desert, then there is another side to the coin. Just because the desert is the ultimate in terms of hopelessness, so it is also the place where salvation can most dramatically be seen. The Bible is full of it. 'In the wilderness shall waters break out'. It is the 'Voice in the wilderness' that prepares 'a highway for our God'. The desert makes us notice things we had never noticed before.

When I was a priest on a large housing estate, I had to cross some really ugly waste land every Tuesday in order to celebrate the Eucharist in an old people's home. In such a tip, a thistle in full bloom stood out in a beauty that normally I would never have noticed. Thomas Merton once rebuked his novices for not having noticed that the desert cactus was in full bloom. There are millions of them to be enjoyed by those who would notice them, he observed, and the only beings which take them in are the rattle snakes.

The Devil, however we interpret that symbol, is keen to tempt us out of the desert. If only we can stay in our most lonely and vulnerable places, it is there that we will most realize that we are desperate for meaning and so for God. Such places can seem terrible at the time but with hindsight are seen to be the making of us. Winston Churchill could talk of his wilderness years only with hindsight. Gethsemane and hanging on the cross were the ultimate desert experiences for Jesus. We see their value only with hindsight. The Gospel story is one told from hindsight.

The Bible is quite clear. We are told that it is the Spirit who leads Jesus into the wilderness, not the Devil. The Devil is rather the one that tries to make Jesus leave. Built into a retreat is the beauty of the place, the opportunity for fellowship and much else. Each of these is, of course, valuable. Otherwise we would be seeking to avoid them. But none of these must be an end in itself. They are aids by which God calls us to listen to him as we seek to discover more about ourselves. Let us renew our confidence that there is something to be heard. 'For in the wilderness shall waters break out and streams in the desert'. So pray big and with expectancy. The desert was a key place for Jesus; may it be the same for us.

Martyn Jarrett has been the Bishop of Burnley since February, 1994.

Who Needs a Spiritual Director?

GORDON JEFF

We live in what has been called a 'problem-centred' culture. Life is assumed to go on without comment until a 'problem' arises. The 'problem' is sorted out and may or may not result in another 'problem' which also has to be sorted out in its turn. Problems beget more problems and many have come to believe that the only time it helps to talk about themselves is when they have a 'problem'. Most counselling is based on the clinical model of a patient needing a cure for a problem of some kind. Counselling also tends to be relatively short-term.

Spiritual direction, however, takes as its starting point a growth model. True, under God we are all sinners, but in Christ we are basically healthy. A spiritual director, I believe, is helped by having a basic competence in counselling and will sometimes have to *be* a counsellor to his or her directee, or to do a bit of counselling (problem-solving!) before being able to get down to the real work. Spiritual direction is nevertheless primarily concerned with the healthy person growing closer to God. It is therefore a longer term affair than counselling, and the relationship will often continue over many years.

I have a dream of a Church in which every practising Christian would talk with someone else at least once a year about how they were getting on in their prayer and faith. We are all different; there are as many ways to God as there are individuals, and although books and sermons can be very helpful, there is really no substitute for a one-to-one discussion.

But what right has any other person to believe himself or herself so wise as to be able to 'direct' another person towards God?

It is true that there have been – and perhaps are – some very directive directors. St John of the Cross said scathingly, 'Not one in a thousand is capable', amended by St Francis de Sales to, 'Not one in ten thousand'.

The only way in which I can use the word 'direction' is by understanding it as two people sitting down in an atmosphere of prayer and together attempting to discern in what direction the Holy Spirit is trying to lead the directee. It is a prayerful and learning situation for both and in my view the director should do no more than offer suggestions or ask the sort of questions which help the directee to understand better.

A spiritual director is therefore not just for the élite, but for every Christian; we should hardly attempt even so simple a task as learning to play the piano only by listening to talks on piano playing or reading books on piano playing. We need individual attention as much in praying as in piano playing.

People sometimes ask about the relationship between spiritual direction and sacramental confession. Spiritual Direction is not solely a priestly preserve; I believe most parishes have lay people who are potential directors, and Tilden Edwards in *Spiritual Friend* – reclaiming the gift of spiritual direction (Paulist Press, New York, 1980) holds that there is often a lot to be said for women having men directors and men having women directors. If the director is a priest, the relationship may or may not include sacramental confession. Some may go elsewhere for formal sacramental confession; not all practise it regularly anyhow, and it would be a misunderstanding if we thought for a moment that spiritual direction was a High Church or Roman Catholic phenomenon. There is a great wealth of wise direction in the Protestant divines of the Reformation and after – men like Richard Baxter.

Christians who belong to prayer groups often find help in the kind of discussion which frequently follows the time of prayer, and there will often be members of the group with the breadth of vision to be themselves wise directors. I use the phrase 'breadth of vision' because we need to be wary of enthusiastic members who may try to press on others a way of praying which is fine for them, but not necessarily right for others. A wise director will respect and understand how varied are the ways of prayer by which the Holy Spirit calls individuals into God.

Let us, then, assume that we have decided we could be helped by having a spiritual director. How do we set about finding one? Let's remember that not all clergy are called to be spiritual directors, while many lay people *are*.

A list of names such as the one held by the Julian Meetings may be of help for some; others may prefer a more personal approach, and we need not be afraid of asking around to find out to whom other people go. Having found a possible person, there is no need to feel committed. Talk through with him or her exactly what you are looking for, how often it might be helpful to meet, and whether or not you are looking for formal (or informal) confession.

Try to discover in this initial discussion whether you are each comfortable with the other and that a good relationship could be built up. No director worth his or her salt will be in the least offended if you say you don't think it feels right, and the director might perhaps say the same to you. Alternative suggestions could well be offered. From there onwards if you both decide to go ahead it is up to the Holy Spirit and to the two of you.

I have often quoted St Bernard's acid remark, 'He who sets himself up as his own teacher becomes the pupil of a fool', because I believe it to be essentially true, and I hope those who read this article who do not yet talk deeply about their prayer and vocation with someone else, may feel encouraged to begin the search for their own director and spiritual friend, and that their search will be rewarded.

In the relationship of direction many of us have come to find not only help on our way to God, but lasting human friendships as well.

Canon Gordon Jeff is a founder member of SPIDIR and author of *Spiritual Direction for Every Christian.* (SPCK, 4th imp. 1993).

Am I Doing it Right?

GRAHAM JOHNSON

A nun once wrote to ask if she could include my name on a list of spiritual directors. I declined as I thought it was wrong to advertise myself. What should I have put: 'Climbed Mt. Carmel 1962. Awarded first prayer stool 1963. Abhishiktananda Trophy in the London (Jesus Prayer) Marathon. Creation Spirituality with just a smattering of St Augustine. Wife makes soul-reviving lapsang tea during interviews (No flagellation involved)'?

I am not sure that one can pick a director from a list. Apart from parishioners or retreatants who have got to know me as parish priest or retreat conductor, all the others who come have been recommended by friends. It is these friends who are perhaps the real directors. They direct people to me not because of what I know but because they think I would be good company for them on the spiritual journey: 'Graham, will you see N. He has just left the Community; he is far too serious; he needs your sense of humour', or 'Can M. ring you; she has been through a hard time; she might benefit from your lighter approach?'

I was also wary of being put on a list with others who see spiritual direction as forcing people into a mould, giving people impossible rules of life or, more likely nowadays, insisting on one spiritual way which is either completely wrong for the sort of person, (too much Ignatius is not best for introspective people) or merely reinforces one side of their person-ality without developing the whole. I am sure that God does not do encores; each one of us is unique.

Looking back, my first spiritual director was recommended by my cousin. He was a Cowley Father, a member of the Anglican religious order of the Society of St John the Evangelist. Later he was described to me as 'the hard man of the C. of E.', though this never came over in my sessions with him. It does seem that those who are hardest on themselves often treat others with great kindness and gentleness. This was so with my next director, a man of steel and few words. I saw these men at prayer and their own lives spoke to me of God. Our sessions together were made up of the giving of information to help me understand myself better, together with what I can only describe as the cutting out of the dead wood that I had accumulated. There was nothing of the 'horror stories' I sometimes hear: 'He told me that I mustn't go to the cinema', 'I had to say Vespers every day', 'I wasn't to go to Free Church services', or 'His director told him to spend two hours a day in contemplative prayer and exercises leaving me look after our maladjusted child'.

From my first experience of spiritual direction with these two men I have learned that I can only be of help to others if I spend time in prayer myself, and I face the reality of life and struggle with it. I also need to be a sort of resource person with a wide knowledge of the map of the Christian life with its many starting points and many routes to and from the Father. Here I find that it is now much harder than it was. Even up to 1960 the path of prayer was fairly well signposted through Bible meditation (Salesians on the soft verges, Sulpicians on the hard shoulder), Affective Prayer (East for prayer ropes, West for rosaries). Then if your passport could be stamped with John of the Cross's three marks of the ligature to the passive night of the senses you were across the border and scouring the secondhand bookshops for spiritual guides to accompany you up Mt. Carmel, with its Teresian Castles to be stormed with Ruysbroeckian Ladders under cover of *The Cloud of Unknowing*, always maintaining the stiff upper lip of English Spirituality!

But since then has come the Beatles and the influence of transcendental meditation, Abhishiktananda and the mantra as the way into prayer for more people, Father Slade, Anchorhold and the revival of dechanet and yoga and posture in prayer, the English Mystics of the fourteenth century and the associated Julian literature, the Jungian influence and Fr. Christopher Bryant, SSJE, the Charismatic revival, John Main, Father Matthew and Martin Israel. Then we were all off to St Beuno's or through the Open Door of the Ignatian revival, Liberation Theology and now Creation Spirituality and the reinstating of Eckhardt, to say nothing of the much greater influence of the other religious traditions of the world. Bookshops are now *full* of spiritual guides.

In addition the world itself has changed. Since 1940 we have been living in a completely new world and it is usually those born after that date who are realising this fact (see Margaret Mead's *Culture and Commitment*). The rapidity of change in our society means that some are looking for a spirituality of escape whilst others join the spirituality jet-set flying from one guide to another ('It's Wednesday this must be Journalling'). 'In the light of all my new knowledge things are beginning to look very dark' (source unknown).

It is interesting to note that only De Caussade with his *Sacrament of the Present Moment* seems to provide a spirituality for all times and all places. In all my times of being of any assistance to others he is my bottom line. This means that our actual meeting together is important. It needs to be relaxed and unhurried for it is a time of revelation to both of us.

It also means that I must see this person as the person they really are and not someone I would like them to be (because then they would fit into the right size boots that would send them speeding up my spiritual ladder). I have found Fr. Bryant's 'Helping people to Pray' a great help. This was published as 'Prayer and Different Types of People', for an appendix to *The Heart in Pilgrimage* (DLT, 1980). It looks at the person's natural strengths and uses these as a basis for prayer, yet also suggests that we need to see the more neglected side of a person so as to build them up to wholeness. Although I see the person as they are I must look forward to the sort of person they will be - 'Here and now dear friends we are God's children, what we shall be has not been disclosed but we know that when it is disclosed we shall be like him because we shall see him as he is' (I John 3.2). I must confess, however, that often especially with women, I need to convince them of the great value they already are, for they either have a very low opinion of themselves or have been presented with such an impossible model of Christian perfection that they see nothing to affirm in themselves.

Do those who come actually grow in the stature of Christ? Am I doing it right?

Well, those who come more than once keep coming back! I only wish those who only came once would return the books I lent them. Many recommend me to others. But do they grow?

It is difficult to give an objective answer because the old landmarks and signposts have disappeared. If becoming more involved with both world and Church is growth; if suffering through standing up for oneself in a difficult marriage, or losing one's job, or living with physical pain, or sticking with a congregation that does not appear to live the gospel, is growth; if struggling with the contradictions of life, breaking down the necessary but temporary images of God, reaching out for more silence in prayer, and succeeding and failing in all these things is growth then they are growing and so am I.

I have long since ceased to believe in going up the spiritual ladder or the Mount of Perfection as if everyday in every way I was getting better and better. It is not linear progression but more a continuing wave-like motion with peaks and troughs through many facets of response and lack of response - going down into the trough through temptation, crisis, ignorance, mistrust, sin, death, but then rising up through blessing, help, sorrow, repentance, forgiveness, resurrection, restoration and joy.

Joy
Restoration
Resurrection
Forgiveness
Repentance
Sorrow
Help
Blessing

Temptation
Crisis
Ignorance
Mistrust
Sin
Death

If I had the eyes to see I might well see the waves of the first diagram from the viewpoint of the Father as:

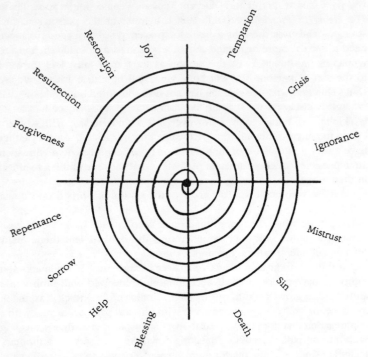

But my vision is limited, and even if I could see in this way I could not be sure whether the journey was inwards or outwards. I would still be left with the question, 'Am I doing it right?'

Intercession

GRAHAM JOHNSON

In the past most English people, when they have thought of prayer, have thought of intercession - praying for others, asking God for things. Often this sort of prayer became a list which told God what to do, though some people left God some leeway by ending with the words, 'but thy will be done.' These prayers were rarely answered so most people soon gave up, though there were a sufficient number of (coincidental?) answers to make people return to intercession in a time of great need.

Of course, in recent times we have seen the growth of contemplative prayer and as the impetus for this came from other Eastern religions, the English have always found it difficult to define what they really mean by contemplation. Unfortunately there is a common belief that contemplation means emptying the mind and thinking about nothing in silence.

I may be parodying these thoughts about intercession and contemplation but I do not think that I am too far from the mark for I still find many people asking how they can contemplate and intercede at the same time 'How can I think about nothing and somebody I want to pray for at the same time?', and in some parishes you will find that there is a contemplative prayer group and another group that prays for others.

It does seem that the hangover of wrong thinking about intercession has built a barrier with the muddled thinking over contemplation. Both ways of thinking are wrong because they are man-centred – what *I* do when *I* pray. Michael Ramsey commenting on the verse 'He ever lives to make intercession for us' said that the Greek word which is here translated 'intercede' does not mean to speak or to plead or to make requests or petitions. It means to meet someone, to be with someone in relation to or on behalf of others. Jesus is with the Father, for us.

I was taught to intercede by focusing on the three great acts of God – the act of creation, the act of redemption and the act of the restoration of all things at the end of the age. This is the teaching that I can remember from the now departed Anglican priest, Father Cedma Mack of the Community of the Resurrection at Mirfield. In following this teaching I have found no contradiction between contemplation and intercession. Sometimes it has been the way into contemplation; sometimes, less frequently, I realise dimly that in the loving attention paid to God, which I think of as contemplation, I intercede as a mystical member of his Son 'by whom all things were made' and that in me are all his longings as the Maker and Owner and Keeper of the world.

Using these three great truths of God to shape our prayer we begin with God as Creator. This means that we begin with praise and thanksgiving. Thanksgiving has been described as *the* Christian prayer. To commence prayer with thanksgiving means that we acknowledge God as the author and giver of life of those for whom we pray. Thank God for all he has done, thank him for other people and situations in your life, thank him for yourself. By thanksgiving these things take on a new value in our eyes.

The second stage in our intercession will be that of presenting before God the causes or those for whom we pray. We are placing a person or situation within the sphere where the redemptive power of God is at work. Such a loving and pure prayer of intercession is extremely costing to us while we are still on earth – for it requires patience, continuity, and the filling of our own hearts with the love of Jesus in order that no merely natural affection, no passing mood of our own may dominate our thought of the person for whom we pray. It is good in this stage of prayer simply to say the name of Jesus over the persons or situations for whom we intercede. They need to have the Name of Jesus named over them as the name that restores, that reconciles with God and with all other men and all other orders of creation.

The third stage in our intercession would be spent in silence in loving attention to God, permitting our Lord, as the restorer of all things and the Consummator of the ages, to place within our hearts His own desires. Our desires are so small and mean . . . His are so great.

Growth in intercession will be marked by simplicity and by the discarding of the many leaflets and lists in the actual moment of prayer – in fact Father Mack said our progress to the steps of the throne of God will seem from above rather like a paper chase. We shall grow less desirous to inform God of his creatures' needs and more eager to be the surrendered wills and loves by means of which he may touch as he wishes all he made and keeps. Such intercession with its final stage of focusing on God as the Consummator of the ages, looking forward to the glory that shall yet be revealed, is akin to the contemplative waiting on God till we see 'good gracious God, His own dear self'.

Techniques of Meditation

GRAHAM JOHNSON

To write about the techniques of meditation is rather like writing a manual of wedding etiquette – no matter how good the manual may be it is useless unless the essential characters, bride and groom, play their part and there is love to bring and bind them to one another.

There is also the danger that, faced with the varying techniques, the reader will think he has set out on an obstacle course in which each technique has to be mastered before passing on to the next. Rest assured that this is no O-level, followed by Degree course. It is simply a grouping together of some of the ways that I have discovered that people have found helpful. The fact that the ways of meditation are put in a certain order simply reflects my own ideas about growth of a normal loving relationship but we all know of people we have met with whom we seem to have a natural affinity and there is little need for those things that often mark the beginning of a relationship – mutual interest and growing attraction. It is not necessary to take what follows as the normal sequence of growth in prayer, rather it expresses three facets of a relationship.

There are many descriptions of the word 'meditation'. If contemplation is described as the prayer of loving attention to God, then, for this writer, meditation is a way of assisting that loving attention. We know that with the best will in the world it is not easy to maintain this loving attention to

God for more than a few minutes (perhaps seconds) before the mind wanders. Over the years certain techniques have been found helpful to encourage our mind and body to assist us in this prayer of loving attention. It is essential to remember that meditation techniques are very simple, especially nowadays when there are so many organisations selling their particular technique and, to attract the customer, turning what could be said in five minutes into long lectures and esoteric teachings.

But although the techniques are simple this does not mean to say that the prayer of loving attention is easy. It demands a discipline of regular practice, a discipline within the time of prayer and a discipline during the rest of the day if the loving relationship is to develop.

Most people prefer to have a regular time and place for their time of prayer. The place may be a church, or a room in the house, or a particular part of a room. It may be in front of a particular picture or religious symbol. Some prefer to sit comfortably, but not too comfortably, in a chair, others to sit in the lotus position, others to stand, others to kneel. Some people find it helpful to hold something in the hands - a cross, beads, rosary - I personally always hold a hazelnut. Some use music as both a preparation and theme for their time of prayer.

To Know You More Clearly

In contemplative prayer we have a privileged share in the ongoing love affair between God and his people. There is no reason why our particular part in this love affair should not develop along the lines of a normal close relationship of love.

First, certain immature ideas have to be dispensed with if any true loving relationship is to be found. The young teenager may wish to go out with someone whose qualities are those of a TV personality, film star, sportsman, tycoon - glamorous, handsome, wealthy. In the same way many see God as their own selfish idea of the person who gives them everything they want, who keeps other people in their place. Hopefully we grow out of these immature ideas about God, though many people do carry them on until something happens to destroy them, such as the death of a loved one, or redundancy or business collapse. Then they either give up God altogether or are forced to rethink their ideas about him. Passing over many intermediate affairs, the time comes when the person begins a relationship with someone that is going to deepen. At first there is the delight of learning about one another as they do things together.

This is rather like one of the techniques of meditation. By coming alongside Jesus in the Gospels or in the writings of others who have been close to him we come closer to Jesus ourselves.

The time of prayer is spent in first reading a passage from the Gospels. Try to picture the scene and imagine that you are there watching what is happening, listening to what is said. Then try to see how it applies to you;

try to enter into its meaning. What demands does it make upon you? Some people then find that it helps to make a simple resolution that you will put into practice during the day – so putting whatever you may have gathered from your meditation into operation.

A simple way of remembering these three steps in this way of meditation is to think of Jesus before the eyes, Jesus in the heart, Jesus in the hands.

There are many variations in this technique. You can read from other parts of the Bible or other spiritual literature. You can read, slowly, well-loved Christian prayers and the words from the liturgy. But in all these things we are coming alongside Jesus and coming to know him better.

To Love You More Dearly

In a fairly normal love affair the need to do things together becomes secondary to the need just to be with that person. When we are with them there is not a great need for talking. We know one another fairly well, we know one another's likes and dislikes. Perhaps we talk softly to one another. Perhaps saying the same thing over and over again. Someone eavesdropping would probably laugh at some of the things we said to one another but to us they are words to be treasured.

The same sort of thing can happen in our prayer. Those who have been regular church worshippers for many years have in fact been using the technique of Jesus in eyes, hands and heart in every service. They may not have known they were meditating but in the words of the gospel, the acts of the liturgy and the preaching of the word they will have been brought to a closer knowledge of Jesus. Therefore in their prayer they will not want to dwell so much on the actions of Jesus in some part of his life but instead will find a single meaningful phrase, repeated over and over again, will hold them in their awareness of God.

This is another of the techniques of meditation – the repetition of a word or phrase, often called a mantra. It may be just the word 'God' or 'Jesus'. It may be a phrase from a psalm or hymn or a saying of Jesus. St. Francis of Assisi used the mantra 'My God and my all'. Many people use the Jesus Prayer, 'Lord Jesus Christ, Son of God, have mercy on me, a sinner'. Others prefer words or phrases from the ancient languages of early Christianity – 'Abba' 'Kyrie eleison', 'Maranatha'. Benedict taught his monks to say, 'O God make speed to save us.'

The mantra is at first repeated over and over again. Then the time between each repetition lengthens, the word or phrase only being repeated when the mind wanders and needs to be brought back in line again. At first we may be concerned with the meaning of the word or phrase but as time goes on it becomes part of us. People who use this technique of meditation discover that the mantra stays with them during the rest of the day and they say it silently as they go about their work. The mantra appears to be taken up by the heart where 'it lives itself in every heart beat.'

To Follow You More Nearly

There comes a time, if the normal love affair is allowed to develop to its full extent, when there is close communion with one another without a word being spoken. We are just happy to be there with the one we love. There is no need for words because we are at one with one another.

This can happen in our prayer. All words and ideas seem superfluous and we are happy just to be there with the Father. It may be that no technique of meditation is really needed but the fact remains that still our loving attention will wander and, though it may be brought back by reading or the use of a mantra, there is another technique which may assist us at this time. For, just as we are content to wait on God, though he is hidden from us, so in some religious symbol there is, hidden beneath what we can see, an inner reality.

'A symbol is a powerful image that focuses the imagination, releases the emotions and moves us to action' Fr Christopher Bryant, ssje once said.

The simplest symbol is perhaps the circle, but Christians have also the cross, water, bread, wine, candle, star, chalice and wedding ring.

By simply looking at the chosen symbol when the mind wanders away from its loving attention, and not trying to understand it or think about it, we hold ourselves ready for when the Father calls us again and we look at the things the world has longed to look into, things beyond our wildest dreaming, into the very heart of God.

As was said in the introduction you may not find the order of the use of techniques to be the order that most suits you. Nor will you necessarily use them in the same way. Some may find that a symbol is enough to hold their attention right at the start; others may wish to think around a symbol and so use it rather like the techniques of meditation on the Gospels, or link the symbol with one of the sayings of Jesus – 'I am the light of the world', 'I am the bread of life' – and use these as mantras.

Many who have practised contemplative prayer for many years still read from the Gospels or some other spiritual work as a preparation for their time of prayer.

It is important to find a wise person with whom to talk about your life of prayer. At first there is an initial enthusiasm which can carry us along. The practice of contemplative prayer can make us feel good and calm, but gradually the going gets harder and we begin to doubt whether this is the right thing for us. In many cases this is just when God is really showing us more of himself but because he is outside our normal thoughts we need to re-educate ourselves in the new ways of understanding him. Unlike the teenager, who usually grows out of his selfish ideas about the sort of person he wants to love, we are constantly picturing God in our selfish way and need to have these ideas stripped from us if we are to see God as he really is. A wise person can help us in this.

There are other things that holds us back in our life of prayer. None of us does the will of God always at all times and often our own stubbornness of will is not apparent to ourselves but quite clear to someone else. Often this stubbornness of will is a cause of the distraction in our time of prayer but there are other sources of distraction and a wise person should be able to point them out to you and explore tactics for dealing with them.

It has also been said that the way of contemplative prayer is not easy. In fact at times it is downright hard, and sometimes boring (there are boring times in any relationship). To have someone who understands, who can help, a 'soul friend' or spiritual guide can be a great consolation, and it can also be of great help to belong to a group of people who regularly practise contemplative prayer.

Graham Johnson is an Anglican priest. He is Warden of Launde Abbey, the Leicester Diocesan Conference Centre, and a member of the Julian Meetings Advisory Group.

The Contemplative Way In Hospital

MICHAEL JOHNSON

The establishment of a Julian prayer group, meeting in a large and busy modern District General Hospital, is something of a novelty. From the perspective of a hospital chaplain, it is an invaluable resource to the institution. I am increasingly conscious of a link between the ministry and witness of contemplative prayer and the role of hospital chaplaincy. Both are concerned with 'being', perhaps more than they are with 'doing'.

Through the life of prayer and meditation, the contemplative seeks to be with God, to 'abide in his love' (John 15:9), after the example of, and through union with, Jesus, who abided in God's love (John 15:10), so that the fruits of such 'abiding' love (John 15:12), joy (John 15:11), peace (John 14:27), faith and confidence (John 14:12), knowledge and understanding (John 14:26) may more consciously and refreshingly be experienced in mind, body and spirit, and shared with others.

'He who dwells in the shelter of the most high, who abides in the shadow of the Almighty, will say to the Lord "My refuge and my fortress, my God in whom I trust." ' (Psalm 91:1)

That a busy modern District Hospital should have an element of the contemplative about it, and provide space to 'come apart and rest', has in the past been acknowledged through the provision of chapels and chaplains yet we have only to look at the origins of the word itself (hospital, hospice, place of rest) to discover that herein lies a very significant constituent in health care. We could be in danger of losing this valuable ingredient if the tide of secularisation, which is marching through the NHS as through other institutions of our national life, under the constant pressure of financial restraints, is allowed to view the spiritual and religious care of people in the future as luxuries which the service can no longer afford.

The earliest hospitals were undoubtedly religious houses and certainly places of rest, refuge, shelter, not only for the sick, but for a whole range of human needs and conditions. Possibly they reflected the semi-monastic tranquility out of which so many of them grew and developed. I suspect, however, that 'tranquillity' is a word seldom applicable to hospital life today. They operate in a highly complex and technological environment, where speed, efficiency and cost effectiveness produce the same 'stresses and strains' which characterise the rest of life in the world today. Add to this an NHS seeking to re-shape itself to cope with the strictures of cutbacks and reorganisation, while at the same time addressing the challenge of higher expectations, and you do not exactly end up with the seed-bed out of which rest and reflection can grow.

Places, like people, have an 'atmosphere' which reflects the sort of activity which is going on within. Hyper-activity, stress and tenseness will hardly be conducive to that spiritual rest which makes possible deep communion with God, and there is a certain fait accompli that large modern hospitals will have more than their fair share of the former. But set in the midst of this *there is still* the hospital chapel . . .

A steady procession of people, not all of them 'church-goers' in the strict sense of the word, will always find their way to it at all hours of the day, or night. Often they will not find it easy to vocalise what they are looking for. I aim to spend as much as I possibly can of the first hour of each working day in the chapel, simply 'being' – calling to mind the presence of God through intercession, Bible study, or silent contemplation and waiting upon God.

Perhaps one ought not to be as surprised as one is by the consistency with which someone will be led into the chapel during these times of 'being'. It might be the relative of a patient who is waiting for news of an operation. Earlier this past week, it was a member of staff soon to go into the administration offices next door for an interview. Only yesterday, a local minister joined us while he waited for a member of his family to receive treatment in one of the day clinics. The worried look on his face suggested deeper burdens of anxiety, which eventually he was able to release within the 'safe' atmosphere of prayer and fellowship.

We are reminded that Julian of Norwich exercised a ministry of counsel and comfort to the burdened and perplexed, from the window of her cell, which arose out of her being close to God. It was this closeness to God, the fact that she abided so deeply in Him, that made people seek her in the first instance – not the fame of her pastoral counselling skills, real as they undoubtedly were. Not everyone who is led to the hospital chapel needs, or is seeking, the help of the chaplains. It is true to say that there are occasions when their involvement would be a positive hindrance! But what chapel and chaplain must seek to create, through the ministry of prayer and meditation, is an atmosphere of spiritual peace and a sense of the presence of God, in order that people may meet with HIM above all else, and so confront themselves in an atmosphere of loving acceptance and safety. The presence of a Julian Group meeting regularly in the hospital is undoubtedly helping to make this a reality.

In his excellent book *The Christian Healing Ministry* (SPCK, updated 1990) Morris Maddocks quotes from Alex Carrell, a Nobel Prize winner in 1912, whose comments about the power of prayer summarise the matter so profoundly:

> Prayer is not only worship, it is also an invisible emanation of man's worshipping spirit – the most powerful form of energy that we can generate. The influence of prayer on the human mind and body is as demonstrable as that of secreting glands. Its results can be measured in terms of physical buoyancy, greater intellectual vigour, moral stamina, and a deeper understanding of the realities underlying human relationships.

Michael Johnson is Whole Time Anglican Chaplain at Pilgrim Hospital, Boston, Lincs. He teaches counselling skills and lectures on 'Spirituality in Health Care' to groups of NHS staff, and convenes a Julian meditation group of 20 or more people from local churches which meets each month in the hospital.

The Spirit of Lindisfarne

JOHN KEMP

I must admit that ever since as a child I was taught to call that period of English history prior to the Norman Conquest 'The Dark Ages', I have never quite been able to rid my mind of a certain picture – reinforced by certain Victorian illustrators – I see desolate moors and fens or rocky promontories, and swirling mists, all in a twilight glow, in which shadowy figures clad in dark brown cloaks or tunics and cross-gartered emerge for brief periods to take the centre of the stage. These figures are larger than life and some of them are suffused with a mystical light. Thus there are Edwin, Oswald, Readwald and Etheldreda . . . Felix, Aidan, Cuthbert and Wilfrid. Place names, too, play a part in my picture to provide an accompanying auditory image – names like 'Isle of Ely', but above all, 'Lindisfarne'. That name has something about it and for me it has always had a numinous quality. For Lindisfarne is the place of Cuthbert and Aidan and the renowned Lindisfarne Gospels. A holy place. A place of pilgrimage.

Lindisfarne is an island or, at least, it is twice a day; for it is cut off by the sea at high tide and, although there is a causeway by which to reach it, this narrow road some two and three quarter miles long is impassable for some three hours before and after high tide. Indeed, it is immersed at high tide to a depth of six feet. One can imagine how remote and inaccessible a spot it must have seemed way back in the sixth century when it first entered the stage of Christian history. Just the place for a monastery. Indeed, it was there in 634 that Aidan and some Irish monks settled and established a monastic community. Aidan had come to Northumbria from Iona in response to the request of King Oswald for some missionaries to come and convert his subjects to the faith. Aidan himself was first Bishop of Lindisfarne and from there he evangelised Oswald's kingdom.

In 664, some years after Aidan's death, Cuthbert, then about 30 years of age, came to Lindisfarne. He became Prior and, though he served the monastery well, he longed for privacy so that he could meditate. So he withdrew to a small islet to the south-west, now known as St Cuthbert's Isle. Later, he retreated to Inner Farne, innermost of the Farne Islands that lie off the coast near Bamburgh. He was recalled from there to become Bishop of Lindisfarne in 685 but after a busy year preaching and teaching as far afield as Carlisle, he resigned the see and retired to Inner Farne where he died in 687. He was buried at Lindisfarne though, and as everyone knows, when the Danes threatened towards the end of the eighth century, the monks exhumed his body and after years of transporting it all round the north of England, they found a resting place for it at Durham.

Lindisfarne; a name to evoke the flowering of the Church in those far off days. For this little island was the power house of the Church in England in the sixth and seventh centuries. Many monasteries the length and breadth of the country were founded from here and from them in turn, missionaries went out to convert the inhabitants of the region to the Christian faith. Rome's mission to Canterbury in 597 and in the person of Augustine was of great importance and lasting significance. But its importance can be exaggerated – excusably so, for in the light of later developments, the Celtic church had to concede to the authority of Rome and that authority was, in this country, focussed in Canterbury.

Yet Augustine was not the first to bring Christianity to Britain. It came with the Romans and survived in the Celtic church. Indeed, it did more than survive; it positively flourished and the Celtic monks were entirely responsible for the evangelisation of the Saxon settlers in the north and, as we have seen, here and there throughout the country. If those Dark Ages were indeed in any sense 'dark', then Lindisfarne was a bright beacon.

It was therefore with some excitement and awe that one day in late July I made my pilgrimage to the island – Holy Island, as it is now more commonly called. The drive across the causeway is quite thrilling in itself and no doubt one of the reasons for the many tourists that the island attracts. One tried to imagine the pilgrims coming to St Cuthbert's shrine, or in the Middle Ages to the Benedictine priory, making their way laboriously on foot across the sand. Their route, different from the present causeway, is marked by a line of poles. On arrival, there is the usual problem of where to park the car. There is a car park in the village itself, but we opted to go down on the dunes overlooking the harbour and near the castle which dominates the knoll at the tip of the island.

Most tourists seem to visit the castle (owned by The National Trust) but as the building is of little historical or architectural interest (it dates from the sixteenth century) and in any case my family and I had come primarily as pilgrims, we made our way to the priory by way of the village. The place was simply teeming with visitors, ambling up the streets, pausing to gaze in shop windows, crowding into craft shops and the like. Several children were sucking lollipops in the shape of St Cuthbert. Our hearts sank. Where was the 'spirit of place' we had come to find? Anyhow, the priory was well worth the visit and, interestingly enough, not crowded. The nave of the priory church is most impressive: a massive Romanesque affair very reminiscent of Durham with its alternating cruciform and circular piers. Standing in the midst of these, or looking at the few remaining night stairs by which the monks came down from the dormitory in the small hours to the church for mattins, it was difficult not to catch a momentary imaginative glimpse of the priory in its mediaeval hey-day. And not so difficult either to recall Aidan, four or five hundred years before, as one gazed up at the impressive stone statue of him on the north side of the Abbey grounds, presiding over it all with his episcopal crook and carrying the torch of truth and love.

But perhaps the spirit of Cuthbert himself was to be found not on Lindisfarne itself, but across on the little islet to which he retreated from the bustle of the monastery and the coming and going of merchants and pilgrims from the mainland. Cuthbert's isle is easily accessible at low tide – provided you pick your way carefully and are prepared for wet feet. Once on it, all is peace and quiet save for the sound of the wind and the harsh cries of the gulls and terns – sounds which would have been familiar enough to the Saint all those centuries ago. When we were there, there were even some eider duck at the water's edge – birds greatly loved by Cuthbert and known to this day as 'St Cuthbert's duck' or, locally, 'Cuddies'. On the supposed site of his shelter there stands a large wooden cross some eight or nine feet tall. It was here, if anywhere, that we felt the holiness of Holy Island. Here, if anywhere, was the 'spirit of place' we had come to seek.

Perhaps to appreciate Lindisfarne fully one would have to live there and be part of it. Twice a day at any rate, even in summer, the islanders have it to themselves and live their lives unencumbered by droves of tourists. For the pilgrim, a night or two's stay would be a distinct advantage, giving time to explore the quieter parts of the island which the day-trippers never find, providing the opportunity too of passing the time of day with the locals. But if it *must* be a day trip, then St Cuthbert's islet is certainly not to be missed.

John Kemp, formerly Principal of the East Anglian Ministerial Training Course, is presently Anglican chaplain in Kyrenia, north Cyprus.

Contemplation and Resistance

KENNETH LEECH

In a paragraph which has become justly famous, Father Daniel Berrigan wrote:

> The time will shortly be upon us, if it is not already here, when the pursuit of contemplation becomes a strictly subversive activity . . . I am convinced that contemplation, including the common worship of the believing, is a political act of the highest value, implying the riskiest of consequences to those taking part.

The rediscovery of the necessary unity between contemplation and resistance, the mystical and the prophetic, is perhaps the central need of modern Christianity. Berrigan sees the need in the United States for a powerful upsurge of spirituality which will redeem a decayed civilisation. 'The American psyche', he writes, 'cannot become the fraternal instrument of world change until it has undergone the dark night of the soul.' Americans have become alienated from spiritual values by technology and the pursuit of power and wealth, and only a renewal of contemplation can heal its sickness.

Yet, Berrigan wrote elsewhere, that '. . . in the derangement of our culture, we see that people move towards contemplation *in despair*, even though unrecognised. They meditate as a way of becoming neutral – to put a ground between them and the horror around them . . . We have a terrible kind of drug called contemplation.'

Such contemplatives, he says, are cut off from social prophecy, and so 'they become another resource of the culture instead of a resource against the culture.' A spiritual quest which is concerned only with the private world of the individual, with the attainment of personal 'enlightenment', can easily be absorbed by the culture. Capitalist society can make contemplation itself into a commodity.

To divide contemplation from prophecy is to damage and maybe destroy both. Berrigan's theme, that they are a unity, is a theme which recurs in many thinkers and writers. In an earlier age, Charles Peguy wrote that everything worthwhile 'begins in mysticism and ends in politics.' From Latin America comes the call for a spirituality of liberation. From a young radical pacifist in the United States, Theodore Roszak, comes the lament that the religious impulse has been exiled from our culture, but also the view that 'it is the energy of religious renewal that will generate the next politics and perhaps the final radicalism of our society.' From some young radical Christians in Britain comes a search for the 'spiritual dimensions to political struggle': 'the re-examination required was not so much a cerebral critique of theology or politics, but a flesh and blood discovery of spiritual roots.' It is with this search for spiritual roots that Thomas Merton was concerned throughout his life.

Merton's significance is that he embodied in himself the spiritual currents and crises of our age. In the person of this contemplative monk and prophet several worlds met: the worlds of the renewed Latin church, of the rediscovery of Eastern Christendom, of the non-violent movement, of the counter-culture, of Zen and the Eastern mystical traditions, of political disenchantment and political revolt. Merton's writings convey a profound experience of the human predicament in the modern world, and it was an experience which paradoxically he gained through monastic solitude. Like an earlier contemplative, Father Alfred Delp, a Jesuit who was in prison in Nazi Germany, Merton believed that solitude was a vital prerequisite for the awakening of the social conscience. Delp had written:

> Great issues affecting mankind have to be decided in the wilderness, in uninterrupted isolation and unbroken silence. They hold a meaning and a blessing, these great, silent, empty spaces that bring a man face to face with reality.

Liberation always begins on the plot of earth on which one stands. 'In solitude, in the depths of a man's own aloneness, lie the resources for resistance to injustice' (James Douglass). On the other hand, a resistance which has not been wrought out of inner struggle must remain superficial or degenerate into fanaticism.

Merton saw the spiritual life as the life of the whole person. He rejected the smug self-assurance of the devout ones who know all the answers in advance, know all the clichés of the inner life, and can defend themselves against all the demands of being truly human. He knew only too well the dangers of bogus interiority, the distortion by which self-study becomes merely the evasion of risk and struggle. Bogus contemplation, as evidenced in many of the fashionable – and profitable – meditation schools, was concerned to avoid conflict and reduce tension.

But Merton emphasised that 'Christian faith is a principle of questioning and struggle before it becomes a principle of certitude and peace . . . The Christian mind is a mind that risks intolerable purifications' (*Conjectures of a Guilty Bystander*, 1966). The desert as the place of struggle and purification was a constant theme of his message, and he once defined contemplation simply as 'the preference for the desert'. For the desert experience was the experience of solitude in which God appeared to be absent. It was the presence of conflict and struggle which distinguished true silence from false. True silence is 'a repeated bending over the abyss', whereas 'a silence from which he (God) does not seem to be absent dangerously threatens his continued presence'.

In Merton's writings there are marked changes from the period of his early works, such as *The Seven Storey Mountain* (1948) and *Seeds of Contemplation* (1949). The early Merton wrote from within and for the Roman Catholic community of the Counter-Reformation. His assumptions were those of traditional Latin monasticism, and his audience were probably for the most part from within the Christian tradition. It was much later that the work of contemplation was consciously related to the work of social criticism, and the crucial element in this was his philosophy of solitude. He held that solitude was essential to the common good, for it was in solitude that people became fully awake. It is this wakefulness, this insight and enlightenment, which preserves religion from fanaticism, and Merton saw fanaticism as the greatest temptation of the modern age.

Merton's understanding of prayer is central to his social doctrine. He defined prayer as 'a consciousness of man's union with God and as 'an awareness of one's inner self'. Self-knowledge, as all the mystics insist, is essential to sanctity, but it is only the beginning. We need to pass beyond 'introversion', beyond the self, to God. Prayer thus liberates us from self, and from all ideas of self. Merton believed that the central concern with self led to the view of God as an object, and therefore eventually led to the 'death of God' ideas. There must be a real transformation of consciousness, he said;

> This dynamic of emptying and of transcendence accurately defines the transformation of the Christian consciousness in Christ. It is a kenotic transformation, an emptying of all the contents of the ego-consciousness to become a void in which the light of God or the glory of God, the full radiation of the infinite reality of His Being and Love are manifested.

Spiritual progress involves the recognition of false ego-consciousness, and Merton links this directly with *individualism* which has dominated Western theology and politics for several hundred years. 'This individualism, primarily an economic concept, with a pseudo-spiritual and moral facade, is in fact mere irresponsibility'. In confronting this false self-consciousness, we begin the process of recovery of the Divine image which is in all people.

What is crucial here is that behind the account of prayer lies a view of salvation as a participation in God, theosis, a doctrine which is at the heart of Eastern Orthodox theology. Merton drew on the great theologians of the apophatic or negative tradition, and in particular on Gregory of Nyssa, in his understanding of our sharing in God's nature. 'God has made us not simply spectators of the power of God', wrote Gregory of Nyssa, 'but also participants in his very nature'. Through the Incarnation, humanity is led into a mystical union which is not exceptional but is the *normal* Christian life. It is ironical that Merton died on the same day as Karl Barth – 10 December, 1968 – to whom such an idea would have been unthinkable. As an Eastern writer, Paul Verghese, has commented, 'A choice has to be made between early Barth or Basil and Gregory of Nyssa'. Thomas Merton identified himself closely with the Eastern tradition in its stress on the taking of humanity into God through the Incarnation, the basis of all mysticism.

Monasticism therefore is not to be seen as a subtle escape from the Incarnation and the common life of humankind, but as a specific way of sharing in the redemption of the world. Monastic prayer is a deep confrontation with the alienation of modernity, and is thus particularly vital to the undermining of illusion and falsehood. Henri J. M. Nouwen wrote: 'Merton understood that the unmasking of illusion belongs to the essence of the contemplative life'. 'The monk', he wrote in a paper given at Bangkok on the day of his death, 'is essentially someone who takes up a critical attitude towards the contemporary world and its structures'. (*Asian Journal*, 1974) He saw the future of the contemplative life to be closely linked with this critical role. 'The great problem for monasticism today is not survival but prophecy.' So others, including many non-Christians, have looked to Merton and to the monastic tradition for a new perspective on political struggle. Daniel Berrigan himself was steeped in the theology of Merton and learned much from him.

Merton's view of the role of the monk in the modern world comes out clearly in his *Contemplative Prayer*, and in his Bangkok paper on Marxism and Monastic Perspectives. In the former work he argues that 'this is an age that, by its very nature as a time of crisis, of revolution, of struggle, calls for the special searching and questioning which are the work of the monk in his meditation and prayer ... In reality the monk abandons the world only in order to listen more intently to the deepest and most neglected voices that proceed from its inner depth'.

The monk, he says, experiences in himself the emptiness, the lostness of humanity but he meets this at the point where the void seems to open out into black despair. But he rejects the way of despair, and through his prayer there comes healing. In his paper at Bangkok, he points out that the monk 'belongs to the world, but the world belongs to him insofar as he had dedicated himself totally to liberation from it in order to liberate it.'

The unmasking of illusion and the liberation of humankind were to Merton essentially monastic tasks, and they drove him from contemplation to politics. Not in the sense that he modified his contemplative role, and began to campaign or to demonstrate: rather, his theological insight became political insight as an inevitable by-product. 'Christian social action is first of all action that discovers religion ... in social programs for better wages,

Social Security, etc., not at all to 'win the worker for the Church' but because God became man' (*Conjectures*). The Incarnation was central to his social and spiritual teaching, and from the Incarnation he derived a fundamentally *optimistic* view of humanity. Like Gandhi, whom he described, 'he believed that in the hidden depths of our being, we are more truly non-violent than violent'. For Merton, the crucial question in the non-violent debate was whether evil was reversible. 'In the use of force, one simplifies the situation by assuming that the evil to be overcome is clear-cut, definite and irreversible. Hence there remains but one thing: to eliminate it.' (*Gandhi on Non-Violence*, 1964)

Non-violence stands or falls on the view of evil. If evil is an irreversible tumor, then it must be cut out, and for this violence is necessary. Merton held that evil was reversible, and can be changed into good by forgiveness and love. But 'only the man who has fully attained his own spiritual identity can live without the need to kill' (*Raids on the Unspeakable*, 1966). So solitude and the inner quest are vital if peace on earth is to be achieved. Yet non-violence is not merely a method of achieving a result. 'Non-violence is not for power but for truth. It is not pragmatic but prophetic. It is not aimed at immediate political results, but at the manifestation of fundamental and crucially important truth.' Merton, following Gandhi, held that non-violence is part of the law of human society, and that violence dislocates the social order. Violence is the law of the beast, non-violence the law of redeemed humanity. So the commitment to a non-violent life-style is a spiritual commitment, for only the non-violent in spirit can practise the non-violent life.

The American pacifist writer, James Douglass, whose thought owes a great deal to Merton, has described the essential unity of contemplation and action in terms of the Chinese symbol of the Yin and the Yang. The earliest Chinese character for Yin was a cloud, while that for Yang was a pennant or banner. In his later years Merton found much guidance and illumination from the Eastern spiritual teachers and especially from Zen. His concern with Zen was no mere fringe interest. It was in Zen that he rediscovered the need to transcend the Western divisions of matter and spirit, subject and object. In order to progress in God-consciousness, it is necessary to lay aside discursive reasoning and thought, and to go beyond the thinking process to the centre of Being itself.

Merton, in a letter to William Johnston, a priest who had also found spiritual renewal through Zen, suggested that the apparent atheism of Zen was probably the rejection of the view of God as an object. He linked the 'void' in Zen with the 'dark night of the soul' of St John of the Cross. In the darkness of contemplation, the idols and limited concepts of God are dissolved, faith is purified, and one is led to a deeper level of knowing in which the individual is transformed and made whole, liberated through darkness and mystery from idols within and without. Thus the truly contemplative soul is a soul who sees clearly, sees too clearly for comfort. In his dialogue with the Buddhist Nhat Hanh, Daniel Berrigan suggests that in a society where the machine seeks to control human consciousness, contemplation must become a form of resistance. Merton held this view. 'A spirituality that preaches resignation under official brutalities, service acquiescence in frustration and sterility, and total submission to organised injustice, is one which has lost interest in holiness and remains concerned only with spurious notions of order (*Conjectures*).

There is a spiritual basis for human oppression, and there are bogus spiritualities which cry 'Peace, peace' when there is no peace. The aim of Christian contemplation is not inner peace, but the Kingdom of God, and this involves struggle and spiritual warfare. Just as the spiritual attack on Nazism came from people who were committed to a deep prayer and ascetical discipline, so Merton held that only the contemplative who had begun to see, through love, with the eyes of God, was able to provide the necessary resistance to evil which could not be deflected. Certainly his own path showed an ever-deepening perception and insight. James Douglass is one of many writers who testify to that:

> It was early in 1965 and the war in Vietnam was coming home, though few really knew it. Merton knew it in his hermitage. He also knew that racism was stuck in the heart of America, when everyone else was singing 'We Shall Overcome'. Tom Merton prayed, listened, and wrote furious essays against the powers of destruction which he glimpsed first of all in himself. Merton seemed to know the way as no one else did.

Kenneth Leech, Community Theologian of St Botolph's Church, Aldgate, London, is the author of many books on spirituality and social issues. His latest is *The Eye of The Storm* – spiritual resources for the pursuit of justice (DLT, 1992), which received the HarperCollins religious book award for 1993.

The Three Ways

BARNABAS LINDARS

Jesus went to the Father by the way of the cross. That is the model for the serious business of Christian prayer. Contemplation is necessary in a world of action, as ours is today. It is not a sideshow to a busy life, but more and more essential as life becomes more active. It is essential for the balance of personality and for maintaining sanity and a sense of direction. And that means the only true sense of direction in the midst of the maelstrom – the direction to God. In all serious prayer we are setting out on the way to the Father. The object can be expressed as union with God.

That can be misleading, if taken to mean a continuing state of spiritual

Westminster.

Westminster
Abbey

River

West:
Bridge

House
of
Parliament

St Margaret Rd

Abingdon
St

Tufton Rd

Gt Peter St

Gt North Rd

Dean Farrar St

Millbank

DS

20th April — Young people
    — 1st reading — epistle.
    — new hymn.
    — Mime.
       Canticle.
       Gospel.

Can we meet <u>Pat</u> re next Sunday's service.

Mag entry
PCC comment.
'Vision' for parish.
Rota continue
~~Shop for Devon~~

awareness somehow different from normal human consciousness. But if we think of it as direction towards God, it brings in the total drive of our lives. There is a great deal of interest in how to pray, but also a great deal of confusion about it. Traditional Eastern approaches make a big appeal to many who feel that the Church has failed at this point. Yet we ought to be aware of the tremendous contribution which the Christian tradition of prayer has made, and can still make, before we turn to other forms.

According to the Christian tradition there are three ways in the spiritual path; the Purgative Way, the Illuminative Way and the Unitive Way. But these must not be thought of as alternative routes. They are rather three divisions of a single journey. But they are not even necessarily successive, for they may be simultaneous to some extent, and to pass from one to the next is not necessarily to discard the previous one altogether.

To gain the proper perspective, though, we consider first the purgative way. For we cannot do better than take Jesus himself as our model. He went to the Father by the way of the cross. That is the clue. If we would set out on the serious business of prayer, we must accept from the start that it is a setting out on the way of the cross. We shall then be prepared to undertake a practical method and a definite discipline. The indispensible discipline is to make time for prayer and to persevere in it, whether it is satisfying or not. The importance of this cannot be emphasised too strongly.

The method to begin with is that of a simple meditation, thinking about a passage from scripture or a mystery of the faith or a desirable virtue, and this is done during the allotted span of your prayer time. All the experts tell us that such a simple, thinking-out kind of meditation should lead to a resolution. This should be a practical lesson which you can take away, what St Francis de Sales calls a spiritual nosegay, or a thought to return to during the day, a truth that quickens the emotions and pleases the spiritual sense, and invigorates the desire to live up to your Christian calling.

Such a method is necessary when you first take up the practice of prayer seriously, for otherwise you don't know what to do with the time and may feel all at sea. But for many people this very soon begins to be unsatisfactory. To be thinking things out stands in the way of just loving Jesus, and the idea of the resolution, which is supposed to leave you with the will directed towards him, cannot be left until the end of the meditation, but is there from the beginning. So simple meditation may soon be replaced by the prayer of loving attention or simple regard.

During this time of the Purgative Way the mind is very active, and it may seem as if you are doing all the work, and that God is doing nothing. But in fact He is training you through the sanctification of your thoughts, so that you may accept the cross, see the value of it, and allow yourself to walk along the road of sacrifice. Jesus went to the Father by way of the cross, and very soon you find you are alongside Him and have a feeling of fellowship with Him. Prayer under these conditions is a partnership with

Jesus. It has its own secret joy. You may well ask why it should be called the Purgative Way, which sounds as if something pretty drastic is going to happen. But that is just the paradox of it. For while the soul is busily working on its loving activity, what God is doing in the soul is best described as a purgation. He is purging the soul of all that hinders growth in the spiritual life. That is why this state of prayer can truly be called, and can be seen and felt to be, a time of progress. For the affections are weaned away from lesser motives and anchored in the will to love and serve God.

If there is a paradox in the Purgative Way, it is even more the case when we pass to the Illuminative Way. Here we pass from what has seemed to be light into darkness, and the illumination is of such a special kind that it cannot be said to remove the darkness or turn it into light. Rather, what happens is that what is *felt* to be darkness is in the end recognised to be light, and so the paradox remains.

Once more, you need to think of a method and a discipline on the one hand and what God is doing in the soul on the other. The method is not very different from the prayer of loving attention, which most of us can reach once we have embarked on the Purgative Way. But there comes a point when the ease and sweetness go out of it, and we can only hold on by sheer determination. We are all a prey to distracting thoughts and a sense of complete uselessness and confusion. So you can see how important the discipline is in these circumstances, which is steadfast loyalty to your rule of keeping your time of prayer, because there is a tremendous temptation to let it go altogether when it seems so useless. The discipline of a rule is essential for the Illuminative Way, and most of us are in the darkness of this state of prayer for a very long time, sometimes for many years.

The method to be used during this time must vary according to individual needs, but basically it is a matter of holding on to a loving attention to God in spite of all the difficulties. Some people find it helpful to use affective prayer – that is the gentle repetition in the mind of a loving phrase which expresses our aim. But the important thing is to bring the mind back to God, whenever we catch it straying, with renewed acts of good will towards Him.

Here it is very important to avoid misunderstanding. It has been pointed out that this way of praying sounds very much like relying on sheer will power, which is exactly what our friends of the Eastern religions say should not be done. Their methods are, above all, methods of relaxing. This is right, for any unnatural straining only leads to disaster. The acts of the will which characterize this time are better described as acts of good will, gentle expressions of a quiet and steady resolve, which goes with acceptance of the darkness. For, as we shall see in a moment, it is as the nothingness is lovingly embraced that the gleams of the Illuminative Way appear.

What we must accept is that the sense of frustration of this time is not only normal, but it is also essential for real progress. We are still going with

Jesus along the way of the cross, and, as in the Purgative Way, the will is being strengthened for the service of God. But God is also doing something else. He is stripping off all falseness in our apprehension of His presence. As soon as we think we can feel His presence, the feeling is taken away. At the same time there is growth in self-understanding, for to be stripped of false pretensions is to discover the truth about oneself.

The nothingness of this way is thus not just negative, but an opening to reality, even though reality still appears to be a gaping void. Because it is reality about God and reality about ourselves, it is a basis for faith. In spite of all the darkness and the nothingness, you do go on loving God. The loving does not stop. It is at this point, when the nothingness is embraced openly, willingly and wholeheartedly, that the first gleams of illumination appear. The darkness itself is mysteriously discovered to be light. And all the time we go about our normal lives and our normal jobs. Nothing is changed except one thing, a thing of immense value for our world: that we know that there is hope for the world, because in the darkness itself there is unquenchable light.

The gleams of light which we have considered are the first adumbrations of the Unitive Way. Having decided that the darkness is good, and that we want no experience unless it is authentic and real, we are content to leave ourselves entirely in God's hands. With Jesus on the cross, the cry of dereliction is replaced by the complete surrender: 'Father, into Thy hands I commend my spirit'. The gleams of light are the moments of deep assurance that, as Julian of Norwich says, 'All shall be well, and all manner of thing shall be well'. And then, according to the masters of the spiritual life, the soul may find itself ravished in an ecstasy of the love of God, and the Unitive Way is reached.

But it is just here that the danger lies. For one thing, such an ecstasy is quite common at a very early stage in the spiritual life, long before the Unitive Way is reached. This may be a kind of call vision, like Isaiah in the temple when the seraphims cried the thrice-holy hymn. (Chapter 6: 1-5), or like Nicholas Ferrar long before he took up his family religious life at Little Gidding. Most spiritual directors have met people today who have had such an experience. It seems like an anticipation of the Unitive Way, but it may be never repeated, and certainly should never be sought. It is for God to give, if he so wills. But then, again, it is doubtful if an ecstasy of this kind should be regarded as the true characteristic of the Unitive Way, even though the great practitioners of prayer, St Teresa and St John of the Cross, certainly seem to have experienced it.

To me, and perhaps to others of a plain and practical turn of mind, the Unitive Way is best expressed, not in terms of ravishing experiences but in terms of a quiet and peaceful union of wills between the soul and God. The Unitive Way can be expressed in terms of assurance. God and the soul are sure of each other. It is the experience of Jesus at Gethsemane. The discipline of prayer remains the same, that guaranteed allocation of time. The method becomes more flexible, and one may do various things during the time of prayer. But there is a still point deeper down, which is fixed on God and never moves. This is, quite simply, fact. For the most important thing about the Unitive Way is that it is utterly free from self-deception. That is why it has to follow the scouring discipline of the long darkness of the Illuminative Way, and that is why there is no such thing as instant contemplation as far as the Unitive Way is concerned.

Only when you know yourself absolutely, and still find yourself loving God, can you claim to have reached this state. Then you don't claim it; you just know it. And you never talk about it. But there is in fact a secret bond between you and others who have reached this point; the fact that both you and they have a common understanding. Of course, that bond is greatest with Jesus himself.

Finally, in this union of wills there is peace. It is not an escape from the world with its trouble and tribulation, but peace in the midst of it all, peace within yourself and peace with God. Jesus said: 'I have told you all this that in me you may find peace. In the world you will have trouble. But courage! The victory is mine; I have conquered the world.'

Brother Barnabas Lindars of the Anglican Society of St Francis was Ryland's Professor of Theology in the University of Manchester. He was widely known as a retreat conductor and spiritual director. He died in 1991.

Sing a Song of Fivepence

ROBERT LLEWELYN

Have you ever thought of saying evensong or compline with a friend on the telephone? Too expensive to consider, you might say. You would be wrong. It can cost you as little as five pence each per night.

Here is how it may be done for evensong. Each of you has a lectionary giving the psalm and bible passages for the evening. You find these in advance. At an arranged time you phone your friend and begin the office. After the introductory versicles and responses you say the psalm together. I find it best for the leader to say the first part of each verse (up to the colon), and for the other to say the second. On nine evenings out of ten you reach the end of the psalm within three minutes. You are allowed three minutes and forty seconds for a unit on a local call after 6pm (or at any time on Saturdays and Sundays), and this costs just under five pence, which includes VAT.

You then ring off, having previously arranged how the next period should be spent. My partner and I find it best to have a twenty minute break during which time each of us reads the Old Testament lesson, the Magnificat and the New Testament lesson to themselves. One may be through with this in under ten minutes leaving a substantial period for silence. The other may like to take almost the whole time on the readings.

Next it is the turn of the other party to phone. The office is taken up with the Nunc Dimittis, and one goes straight through to the end. This occupies about three minutes allowing for a brief talk before the unit is up. Intercessions can be added before the grace in which case an extra unit will be needed. Altogether you will have had about 30 minutes joint prayer for 10 or 15 pence shared between you. Weekly cost: less than 50 pence per head.

If instead you say compline you arrange for a period of silence during the office (if desired) placing it at an economical point. The rosary or Jesus Prayer may at another time be said if that is your style. Matins can be said on a plan similar to that of Evensong. But for cheap rates, unless at weekends, you will have to be through by eight in the morning!

But there is a problem. You will find it easier if you have your hands free for an office. So if you wish to take this up in a serious way it is best to invest in a special phone for the purpose. Your local BT shop or dealer will be able to tell you about phones which have a built in microphone and loudspeaker. They can cost as little as £25. For those unfamiliar with this sort of phone I should explain they can also be used with the handset only (and microphone and loudspeaker cut off) just as an ordinary phone. However, since the rosary can be worked easily with one hand, rosary style prayer needs the normal handset model only. So, too, any prayer or psalmody known by heart.

The plan has great potential. There must be very many who find it difficult to observe the daily discipline of prayer on their own, but who would welcome this nightly aid with a like minded companion. It could be something really to be looked forward to by elderly and lonely people, and a constructive contribution both to their prayer life and one's own. Many have phones by their beds making the plan equally possible in sickness, the prayer and psalmody then being left to the fit partner alone. Clergy might find pastoral possibilities in the scheme to the benefit of parishioners and themselves.

Especially relevant might the plan be to members of Julian Meetings in helping them to extend the periodical group silence along some regular plan. The twenty or thirty minutes silence could be observed between brief opening and closing prayers or psalms.

'Won't it be thought a bit gimmicky?' said my friend to whom I explained it today. 'The Samaritans may have seemed like that at first' I replied. 'But this could be seen as going one better than they. Whereas their scheme is designed to pull you out of the river, this one is to prevent you falling in'.

Watering the Roots

ROBERT LLEWELYN

I recall watching a television programme devoted to meditation in which a doctor offered the opinion that if as a country we all practised meditation, daily consultant's visits would be cut by seventy-five per cent. A few weeks later another doctor wrote to the *Church Times* saying much the same thing. Some may question the figure but no Christian is likely to quarrel with the principle.

It is an arresting thought and leads inevitably to the reflection that if, instead of clamouring for more money to be put into our Health Service, we were as a nation to take responsibility upon ourselves, turning to our spiritual roots, seeking to draw upon the resources God makes freely available to us, it might be that the health grant could be cut by more than fifty per cent and we would at the same time enjoy the best Health Service in the world. Not that we are called to turn to prayer to help the Health Service! It is a case of seeking first the kingdom of God and the rest being added. (Matthew. 6:33) And many, too would be the additions beyond the region of health, reaching right into the heart of our national life.

Our torn and disordered emotional lives place strains upon our bodies which they were never intended to bear. As that place of healing, the Burrswood Community puts it: 'Failure to respond to the Love of God creates disharmonies and negative emotions such as anger, resentment, envy, fear, despair and selfishness . . . which in turn leads to disease.' And, it has to be added, to excesses of all sorts in the endeavour to find relief from our dis-ease, which excesses in their turn take further toll upon our health and general well-being.

'Failure to respond to the Love of God.' How better to describe Christian meditation than the expression of our desire to be open and responsive to God's love! The Julian Meetings with their emphasis on contemplative prayer are pointing the way to the recovery (or more accurately, perhaps, discovery) of the spiritual dimension in every sphere of life. Yet only a very few Church members are ready for the extended silence of a Julian group. What we need, I believe, in our Anglican Church is a practical way into silence. Daily Offices are one such way, but it is unrealistic to expect many will become regular in their use. Roman Catholics have the advantage over us here. Their rosary, now returning to greater use after a period of decline following Vatican II, is a convenient and practical devotion nourishing the spiritual life at its roots. For, as Carlo Carretto tells us: 'The rosary belongs to that type of prayer which precedes or accompanies the contemplative prayer of the spirit.' Moreover, no books are needed and the rosary itself can be carried with us wherever we go.

My own belief is that we Anglicans need a rosary style devotion suited to general use amongst our own members. I do not mean that it should be exclusive to ourselves but rather that it should be open to all traditions to adopt as they wished. The actual instrument of the rosary would have to be that of the Roman Catholic Church for none other is readily available. Only the prayers on the decade beads would be different. The frame would be the same but the picture changed.

I say this because it is not practical to invite, with any measure of success, Anglicans other than a small minority to recite the Hail Mary; though those who do so should continue in their way. Some have difficulty with the invocation of the saints, and for others 'Mother of God', though designed to point simply to the divinity of Jesus, is a difficult phrase suggesting that the Holy Trinity itself was begotten of the virgin mother. I value the Hail Mary myself but am realistic enough to know it would be unacceptable to most of my fellow Church people. It is true that both difficulties are overcome if, as was common a hundred years ago, the final clause of the Hail Mary were omitted. But that would mean losing the valuable intercessory element as well.

What devotion, then, should be used? I believe that the creed on the cross or crucifix should remain. So too the Our Fathers which introduce the decades and the Glorias which close them. On the decade beads a variety of choice should be possible. At the same time there should be one common foundation prayer taught and practised, and variation as required should open out from there. Not that too much variation is desirable for it takes years rather than weeks or months for a new form of prayer to be firmly lodged in the heart.

If the Hail Mary is not suitable, how about the Jesus Prayer? I have used that myself for a much longer period than the Hail Mary but I think it belongs to the Orthodox rather than ourselves. Not that I would wish to draw anybody away from a devotion which may continue to feed them until the end of their lives. The prayer I suggest has a similar structure to the Hail Mary but is centred directly on Jesus. 'Blessed be Jesus, true God and true man; blessed be the name of Jesus: Jesus, son of Mary, have mercy on us, now, and at the hour of our death.' Here is a prayer expressing praise and petition, which is theologically right, possesses dignity of language, flows easily, and (importantly) has good resonance. The first thirteen mysteries could be the same as in the traditional rosary: the last two might be the Eucharist and the communion of saints.

Catholics are not tied to the Hail Mary in the use of the rosary and there is no need for us to be tied to the above form. Thus a rosary, drawing on well known scriptural words might run: 'Grace, mercy and peace from God the Father and our Lord Jesus Christ: show us your mercy, O Lord, and grant us your salvation'. Or, drawing on the psalms, a rosary of praise: 'O let my mouth be filled with your praise: that I may sing of your glory and honour all the day long'. These and other forms need not be linked with mysteries as in the traditional rosary.

What is needed is a pattern of prayer for daily use with potential for some variation which parish clergy should be able to put realistically to at least a group within their congregations. The point to be emphasised concerning the rosary is, that assisted but not governed by its mechanical dimension, it clears away the surface distractions of the mind setting it free to rest in God. A learner driver is hardly free to talk to a companion, but once the mechanics of driving have been absorbed communication follows easily enough. Our communication in the rosary is with God and his saints.

First of all the rosary works at the relatively superficial level in holding before the mind material (the actual words or the mysteries) for simplified meditative reflection. Later (and much more importantly) it frees the mind for engagement at the deeper subliminal level where the emerging, unfolding deeper self is encountered and new energies of the Spirit are released. Here we are taken to the threshold of contemplative prayer. I believe there are very many waiting to be nourished in some such way as I have described.

The rosary is not a magical incantation. It springs out of the life of the Church enabling its ministry of word and sacrament to take a deepening place in the heart. Bearing this in mind, if ever growing numbers of Christian people would say the rosary daily with such love and devotion as was given them – God asks no more – a surge of new spiritual life would be released in Church and beyond. I am not meaning to imply that the rosary is the only way but rather to emphasise the importance of growth towards the contemplative life which it has always been its function to encourage. To this end I know of no better way than the rosary, traditional or otherwise, whose use is simple, practical and convenient. As corruption, secularism and false values in the families of a nation ultimately make their pernicious influence known in every sphere of national life, so must truth and goodness in the homes, the fruit of all prayer which is genuine and sincere, make its impact at every level.

Our nation is as a tree partially stunted at the roots. In our Welfare State we spend an enormous amount of time and energy in cultivating the branches. It is the predominant work of the Church to direct our energies to the cleansing and watering of the roots. Work on the branches will remain but the tree will blossom as never before.

Robert Llewelyn, formerly Chaplain at the Julian Shrine, now lives in retirement in Norwich. He is the author of several books, the most recent being *Our Duty and Our Joy* (DLT, 1993)

Waiting and Wanting

MICHAEL McLEAN

A well-known credit-card company used to commend its service with the slogan: 'It takes the waiting out of wanting'. It seems to me to sum up the prevailing attitude of our generation. We want our goodies now, whether we can afford them or not; we want perfect relationships without the effort of working at them; we want instant food, instant communications, even instant church-unity, and yes, I fear, instant prayer. The flood of books about prayer, constant lectures, talks and schools of prayer, an almost athenian lust for gurus, indicate a common thirst to pray better. And that is largely good, but it also perhaps indicates an unwillingness to wait in our wanting.

Some time ago one of England's most unknown yet, I think, most influential, figures died: an anchoress who for well over forty years had lived alone in a small hut. No newspapers, no wireless or television, no contact at all with 'the world' except through a tiny handful of people. As one of that highly privileged group I can vouch for her normality and sanity and humour and, above all, for her sanctity. A few days before her death she sent me Christmas greetings from her sick-bed, concluding with the wry and wistful words: 'I'm afraid I'm going to get better again'. But this was not to be. Her living had reached its fulfilment; death gave way to life. Sad though we were, her funeral was the most marvellous joy. It was what she had been waiting for so long.

Those long decades of waiting were rarely easy. Few lights in prayer (at least in the latter years when I knew her), much suffering, loneliness, temptation, doubt, dereliction, helplessness. But she was totally obedient to her vision and rare vocation. Her life and her prayer were simply oblation – an offering to God, for people, in a silence, not only of the lips but of the heart, the mind and the will. It was an ever-growing poverty, a deepening space for God.

Carlo Carretto writes: 'I have had plenty of time to discover my poverty. The meeting with Jesus in the gospel taught me acceptance of this poverty. The meeting has not always been easy: darkness, nausea, dryness, desire to escape, but I have remained, sustained by hope. And I have waited. For me, to pray means to wait. On the frontier of my limits, in the tension of my love, to have the strength to wait'.

In 'East Coker' the poet T. S. Eliot writes, echoing many mystics: 'I said to my soul, be still, and wait without hope for hope would be hope for the wrong thing; wait without love for love would be love of the wrong thing; there is yet faith but the faith and the love and the hope are all in the waiting. Wait without thought, for you are not ready for thought: So the darkness shall be the light and the stillness the dancing.'

This all sounds rather lofty stuff perhaps; the stuff of anchoresses, mystics, poets, the advanced in prayer. But it seems to me to point us to the easiest and the best form of prayer, for many ordinary people. To wait: knowing one will be hopeless at it, helpless in it, sometimes angry, frustrated, fraudulent, bored, empty, useless; but to wait. It is wholly liberating. It makes one realise we do not say *our* prayers, make *our* prayers, but that we enter into *the* prayer of the whole Christ in the whole Christ through the whole Christ.

It will often demand patient effort to wait, even though we feel strangely caught and attracted by it. Perhaps Mary at the foot of the cross is the greatest icon of it. 'Patience' is closely related to 'suffering'. It will require the painful and liberating acceptance of the fact that we have no words, need no thought, that even a technique to hold us there is only an expression of the will to love.

I believe that this is the greatest thing about Lady Julian - greater even than the message she transmitted to us through *Revelations of Divine Love* - that she was prepared to wait. 'I saw him and I sought him; I had him and I wanted him.'

Michael McLean served for 12 years in the parish of Parmentergate where the Cell of Julian of Norwich stands. He was a Canon Residentiary of Norwich Cathedral from 1986 to 1994 and still lives in the city.

Finding Peace at Pleshey

PETER MORRIS

The year is 1932. The scene is the House of Retreat at Pleshey, a picturesque and historic village in rural Essex. The Warden of the house, Lucy Menzies, sits at her desk composing a circular letter of appeal. She writes 'It is a matter of great thankfulness that more space in chapel is so urgently required and that Pleshey is coming to be regarded as a spiritual powerhouse in the life of the diocese and beyond it.' She encloses with her letter a drawing of the new chapel and asks for a 'hedge' of prayer around the work of the house.

In the following year, just over half a century ago, this 'matter of great thankfulness' was crowned by the dedication of the present chapel which celebrated its Golden Jubilee with a festival Eucharist presided over by the sixth Bishop of Chelmsford. At the original dedication the third Bishop closed the ceremony with a petition that this new house of prayer might be filled with the holy spirit of tranquillity and peace.

The fulfilling of that petition has been a matter of great thankfulness for considerably longer than half a century. The site of the House of Retreat and its environs was a distinctive place of prayer as long ago as the fourteenth century when Thomas, Duke of Gloucester, founded a College of Augustinian Canons on what came to be known as 'The Holy Land'. They lived out their rule of worship and service for over 150 years fostering an ideal of spirituality in this peaceful place and undertaking the cure of souls in the parish. Although the life of the College ended with the Dissolution under Henry VIII, the tradition of Pleshey as 'The Holy Land' lingered. It did not end.

The present House of Retreat was built by a Cistercian community of Anglican nuns in 1908. They called their convent significantly 'House of Prayer' and for the next decade upheld within it (the first chapel was in an upper room) the atmosphere of tranquillity and holy calm which has continued to encompass all who come into it.

One of the great figures in the life of Pleshey between the wars was Evelyn Underhill, mystic and teacher of prayer. She found in the house and garden a setting of established spiritual peace and she was delighted to conduct retreats here leading people via the silence of Pleshey into the peace of God. For her Pleshey was a 'thin' place – that is a place where the barrier between heaven and earth, time and eternity is thin and easily penetrable. Such a place Pleshey has been and continues to be. That is why the use made today of its comfortable accommodation and pleasant garden is primarily for silence, prayer and contemplative awareness and seldom for conference and discussion.

The house owes its existence to our inherent need of prayer and worship. It was built for a community whose chief work this was. The ground it stands on is holy ground from which prayer has gone up for hundreds of years. Today it preserves its atmosphere of peace and serenity. Its worship is offered in a chapel newly re-ordered to meet the needs of today's liturgy and today's visitors. Many, of all ages and from all walks of life, still find in Pleshey the joy and peace and refreshment that comes from closer communion with God in silence.

Before retiring to Westleton in Suffolk, Canon Peter Morris was Warden of the House of Retreat and Vicar of the parish of Pleshey.

A Sign Following

JAMES NATERS SSJE

At the end of St Mark's Gospel we hear our Lord saying 'These signs will accompany those who believe: in my name they will cast out devils; they will speak in new tongues . . . they will lay their hands on the sick, and they will recover.' In the Church today we are seeing a recovery of the ministry of healing, and a deeper understanding of the ministry of deliverance; but what about the sign of speaking in new tongues?

St Paul lists gifts of the Spirit (1 Corinthians 12:4–11), and amongst these gifts is speaking in tongues. It is only one of the gifts, but it does seem to be a very basic gift, which is frequently mentioned in the New Testament, and when the first Christians were baptised in the Spirit at Pentecost they immediately began to speak in new tongues (Acts 2:4) In the house of the Roman Centurion Cornelius, as Peter was preaching 'the Holy Spirit fell on all who heard the word. And the believers from among the circumcised who came with Peter were amazed, because the gift of the Holy Spirit had been poured out even on the Gentiles. For they heard them speaking in tongues, and extolling God' (Acts 10:44–46).

At Ephesus Paul met twelve disciples of John the Baptist, and he baptised them in the name of Jesus; 'and when Paul had laid his hands upon them the Holy Spirit came upon them; and they spoke with tongues and prophesied' (Acts 19:6). Finally a word from the fourth century Church: St Augustine says, 'We shall do as the Apostles did when they laid hands upon the Samaritans and called the Spirit on them. In the laying on of hands it is expected that the converts should speak with new tongues'.

So, what about the gift of tongues? This particular gift of the Spirit is so often misunderstood that I have been asked to write about it from my own experience. For me, quite a long time elapsed between a renewal in the Spirit and speaking in tongues. I was quite prepared to accept the gift if God wanted to give it to me, but I was not at first prepared to ask specifically for it; this is a mistake which probably many people make. After two or three years various friends told me that in their own lives, and in their ministry, speaking in tongues gave a new dimension and was a real strength; and so I too began to ask for this gift, and friends prayed with me that I might receive it. Nothing very much happened!

About this time Jackie Pullinger, that remarkable young missionary in Hong Kong, author of the book *Chasing the Dragon*, was in England and came to see me; Jackie prayed with me for this gift, and suggested that I must work at it, beginning just to make noises in my prayer until I was given the prayer language God meant me to use; moreover she suggested that I do this for half an hour each day. I didn't do very well at this, and soon gave up trying! It was about a year later that I went to the annual Anglo-Catholic Charismatic Convention at High Leigh, Hertfordshire and there, at the very first meal, tea time, I happened to sit next to a complete stranger, who, out of the 200 people there, was a personal friend of Jackie Pullinger and had recently been with her in Hong Kong – God has his way of arranging things! So of course I spoke of my neglect of earlier advice about speaking in tongues. During that Convention I was much helped, and the climax came on the last day. I awoke with a heart full of praise and thankfulness that morning, and was longing to be able to express this praise more adequately in a new language. Quietly a phrase, only seven or eight syllables, came into my mind, and I spoke it aloud, over and over. In the days ahead I quietly went on using this phrase, and gradually the language increased as I became more fluent.

It has seemed worthwhile to share this personal experience with you, because it highlights the fact that the gift of tongues does not necessarily come spontaneously - even after we have asked for it - and with many of us it is something we need to work at. There *are* times when the gift comes spontaneously, even unexpectedly; recently I prayed, with laying on of hands, with a member of a religious community who was longing for the gift of tongues. This person then went to her room and began reading a book, not at that moment expecting anything, when suddenly a new language welled up within her and she found herself speaking in tongues. Yes, sometimes it does happen like this; at other times God wants us to work at it, trying to pray with words that are not our own language, until eventually the new language is given - and we should persevere with a set time each day.

For most of us the gift of tongues is a prayer language. There *are* cases when in a group of people someone may be inspired to give a message, or a prophecy in an unknown tongue. St Paul tells us that when this happens there must always be someone there to interpret the message. But it is as a prayer language that most of us receive the gift of tongues, a gift which gives us a new depth and a new freedom in our prayer. Primarily it is a prayer of worship and praise, a way that goes beyond the restriction of ordinary language, and can take us deeply into adoration and wonder in the presence of God.

It is also a helpful way of intercession. So often we don't know what are the deepest needs of those we pray for, so we place them in God's hands, praying for them in tongues, praying in the Spirit. 'For we do not know how to pray as we ought, but the Spirit Himself intercedes for us with signs too deep for words. And he who searches the hearts of men knows what is the mind of the Spirit, because the Spirit intercedes for the saints according to the will of God ' (Romans 8:26-27). Quite often when I minister to someone with the laying on of hands I do pray in tongues, and it is the experience of many that this is a very powerful kind of prayer.

Adoration, intercession - and contemplation. Usually we think of contemplation as being silent, but I find that contemplative prayer is helped by looking and using, quietly within myself, the language of tongues. Certainly speaking in tongues is a great aid to recollection, and so can lead into contemplation. But more than this, it can be part of contemplation itself.

'These signs will accompany those who believe . . . they will speak in new tongues.' This gift is very basic, it is usually the first gift to be received, and it is often the key to some of the other gifts. Surely God wants us to use his gifts with joy and thankfulness, and we need to be ready to *ask*, as Jesus told us to. Here in the promised gift of tongues is a gift which can help our prayer to grow and deepen, a gift in which we find a new freedom, a gift which brings great joy in its use; and above all it is a gift which we receive and use to the glory of God who gives it.

Renewed in God's Spirit

JAMES NATERS SSJE

One of the exciting things today is the way in which springs of living water are welling up in different areas of spiritual experience; these living springs produce streams which often overlap, and can then flow on as a powerful river for the healing of the nations. Two such springs are the growing involvement in contemplative prayer, of which the Julian Meetings are a manifestation, and the charismatic renewal which is leading so many Christians to a deepening awareness of God in their lives. As I share something of my own experience of renewal with you, you may well consider whether charismatic renewal has something to offer to those of us who are called to the prayer of contemplation.

For me, charismatic renewal was a gradual process, and I can see several milestones on the way. An early pointer was David Wilkerson's book *The Cross and the Switchblade*, lent to me many years ago in South Africa by Mother Mary Eleanor of the Community of the Resurrection. Then there was a talk by Michael Harper, given in our house to the Cowley Clergy Chapter; Michael is one of the leading Anglicans in the renewal, and he gave me for our library *Nine o'clock in the Morning* by Denis Bennett, a book which helped me greatly. By this time I was ready to ask for a special outpouring of the Holy Spirit for renewal in my life; others also prayed with me, and I began to find my life growing in a new depth.

Prayer became more 'real', and there was an even greater desire to praise God - adoration and praise is one of the distinctive marks of charismatic prayer groups. The Bible spoke more directly than before, and psalms and canticles in the daily Office were often lit up with new meaning. The healing ministry, which has always meant much to me, was deepened, and now there was added emphasis on inner healing. And I felt a longing to share prayer and praise, and to share the experience of renewal, with other Christians. In this experience of newness of life a great support was a shared prayer group which I began in Oxford - we do need the support of others as we grow in the Christian life.

There are some people who can look back to a particular moment when the Spirit was given for renewal, and others like myself for whom it has been a gradual process. But all can look to this gift of God with a deep humility, thankful for the love and goodness of God who makes all things new.

What is often called the charismatic movement describes a renewal in which congregations, communities, individuals, seek to be open to the Holy Spirit. Why 'charismatic'? Because when people really are open to the Spirit remarkable things happen, and some of the charisms, or gifts, known amongst the earliest Christians begin to be manifested. In 1 Corinthians 12:4-11 St Paul speaks about the various gifts of the Spirit: wisdom, faith, healing, working of miracles, prophecy, discernment, and of course the speaking in tongues and interpretation of tongues about which I have already written (A Sign Following, page 115). We are beginning to see *all* these gifts manifested in different parts of the Church today. We need hardly be surprised at this rediscovery of the gifts of the Spirit, for Jesus tells us 'he who believes in me will also do the works that I do; and greater works than these will he do, because I go to the Father' (John 14:12)

It is not the gifts, however, which are of first importance. Rather it is the renewal itself in which lives are changed and, as with the first Christians, people are given a new awareness of the living Lord, and a new awareness of each other. Openness to the Holy Spirit is today issuing forth in that quality of life which we read about in the Acts of the Apostles, with its special note of praise and joy: 'With one mind they kept up their daily attendance at the temple, and breaking bread in private houses, shared their meals with unaffected joy, as they praised God and enjoyed the favour of the whole people' (Acts 2:46-47).

In 1975 there was a conference of ten thousand Roman Catholic charismatics in Rome, which culminated on Whit Monday in a High Mass at St Peter's when eight hundred priests concelebrated. In his sermon Pope Paul VI spoke words which could well form a point of meeting between charismatic renewal and contemplative prayer today: 'We desire that Christians, believing people, should experience an awareness, a worship, a greater joy, through the Spirit of God among us.

James Naters ssje is the Superior of the Society of St John the Evangelist, widely known as the Cowley Fathers.

The Priest as Contemplative

PETER NOTT

'Do not rush into speech, let there be no hasty utterance in God's presence. God is in heaven, you are on earth: therefore let your words be few.' (Ecclesiastes 5:2)

That is not advice which comes easily to us. Words pour out of us week by week in sermons, talks, visits, discussions and meetings. Month after month words flow from our pens, rather jerkily, for the magazine. We rush into speech at the least provocation: we utter very hastily before God, especially if it has been a difficult week. God is in heaven and we are on earth, and our words are many. We produce them by the hundred thousand, undisciplined like an undamned flood. If there are pearls among them they easily get lost in the muddy, swollen stream. Did you know that the average Church of England clergyman, preaching two ten-minute sermons each Sunday, produces the same number of words as the entire New Testament every eighteen months? We are professional producers of words, and we are highly over-productive!

In very sharp contrast to this is the ministry of Jesus. Given that the gospel writers were selective, even so one gets the clear impression that Jesus was not in fact a man of many words. For the most part his sayings are short and succinct; his stories brief and to the point. Even in those last few days which were so closely observed, the gospel writers between them can muster only a dozen short sentences uttered by Jesus. And of course his sayings have for us a depth altogether in contrast with the words we produce.

What is it that lies behind this economy with words? Why is it that his words have such power and his images appeal so convincingly? Humanly speaking what is his expertise? I believe it is the art of the contemplative. In order that we may learn how to handle words properly, it is necessary for us to learn the art of contemplation. By that I mean something rather broader than contemplation as a particular and special kind of prayer. It is a combination of elements of silence and concentration, which applies to a great deal more than prayer. I can best explain what I mean by citing one or two examples.

We are perhaps most conscious of our verbosity in our pastoral encounters. We must all have had the experience of regretting an interview in which we know we have spoken too much and listened hardly at all. In meetings, in PCCs, over and over again it is the unnecessary word which has ruined things – hardly ever the lack of a word. Yet we probably also know the marvellous experience of being ministered to by silence. A priest I used to consult regularly was like this. I cannot remember anything much of his words. But I vividly remember his silences. He would listen, perhaps ask one or two questions, and say very little. In an interview with him long periods were spent in silence. Getting an opinion out of him was almost impossible. Yet somehow in his silent presence one's problems were put into perspective. He did not speak much but just because he kept quiet perhaps God did speak.

In our ministry we all know the occasions, especially during bereavement visiting, when we simply have no words to say. We hope that in those moments the Holy Spirit will come to our aid. I believe he often does by giving us the courage to say nothing. We think of speaking in tongues as invariably something audible. It is at least possible that the voice of the Holy Spirit speaking through us may be a silent voice, using words, imparting healing, at a depth and in a way quite undetected by human faculties.

This silence, through which God communicates, does not come easily. Our natures and our surroundings militate against it. And silence is not a gift some people have and others do not. It is an art that must be practised. This is why the narrower definition of contemplation as a form of prayer is so vital. To practise stillness in our prayer is the only way to achieve a silence which will instinctively become part of our ministry; a silence through which God can communicate. It is not easy, for our prayer tends to suffer from the same wordiness as afflicts us in other areas, and we do need to rediscover the place of stillness in both our daily prayer and in our liturgy.

The words of Jesus are measured and profound. They have an eternal depth because they are spoken by a man who clearly spent long periods in contemplative stillness. This is why his words become the Word, the vowels and consonants charged with the life of God himself. His words are spoken out of a depth of inner stillness, not, as so often with us, from a bustling noisy interior. But there is more to contemplation than silence alone. It is a combination both of silence and concentration, or attention.

It seems obvious that concentration should be central to our ministry, but it is as we know not always easy. The multitude of things we have to do and people with whom we are concerned makes concentration difficult. The pace with which we are expected to conduct our lives does not make for concentration as a natural faculty. Like silence, it is not a gift but an art to be practised.

The person who probably knows most about contemplative concentration is the artist. Even the amateur knows this by his experience. I am not an artist, but I have dabbled from time to time, though I became greatly discouraged a few years ago. I rashly and conceitedly framed a water-colour of a fishing village and hung it on a wall. A visitor who knows about these things, came in and went up to it and exclaimed: 'I say, a Cornish Primitive – how quaint'. But, despite a lack of artistic ability, one knows the experience that, having once tried to draw a tree or a face, however badly the attempt has turned out, you never look at a tree or a face in the same way again. Drawing and painting teaches you how to look, how to concentrate the attention and you become aware of things and people in new ways. The artist becomes absorbed in the object, and during intense concentration becomes aware of light and shade, shapes and colours, depths – that are never open to the casual glance.

The point is this. It is not enough to gaze at a scene: the artist looks with great intensity and concentration. It is not enough to be merely silent with a person: there must be a certain intensity of listening and inner reflection for the silence to have depth. Contemplation is not the passive quiescence some believe – it is very hard work.

Of course we have to accept that to learn this kind of concentration means a certain limiting. We cannot be concerned with a multitude of things and people all at once. We have to be convinced of the truth that the quality of our work matters more than its quantity. This is no easy matter in a society which measures worth by the amount of money someone earns, the number of their possessions, or the quantity of things produced. And, unfortunately, we clergy are sometimes no different, for we preach justification by faith week by week and daily justify ourselves by the amount of work we do. But contemplation is not possible unless at the same time quality and not quantity has supremacy.

The infection of stillness in our life and ministry only comes through the persevering practice of stillness in prayer. Similarly, the art of concentration comes only through this means. Here again we must be committed to the truth that it is quality that matters. The intensity of concentration that I am talking about cannot be maintained for long periods. Those who have experienced worship at Taizé will know what I mean by intensity in prayer. On our first visit a member of our party asked one of the brothers why they didn't pray more often or for longer periods. The offices there are only three a day and quite short – not really comparable with most monastic communities. The answer to our question was that the brothers worked for their living. They could not have the time for prayer that other communities with other life-styles had. But, said the brother, we try to make the maximum use of every moment we spend in prayer. This is one reason why the worship at Taizé is so magnetic – there is an intense involvement of everyone there.

If we are to teach laity to pray with any realism, then it is precisely in this area that we need to focus. We need to speak far more of quality and intensity, and less of rules of life which involve commitment to impossible quantities of prayer. And we cannot successfully teach prayer in this way unless we ourselves know it by experience.

Acts 20:28 contains St Paul's famous charge: 'Keep watch over yourselves and over all the flock of which the Holy Spirit has given you charge.' On re-reading this passage, I thought it would be good for me to look at the Greek. I must confess it is not a thought which comes as often as it should. But virtue was rewarded, because in fact the word for 'keep watch' is interesting. It is not *phulassein*, in the sense of guarding or watching over, but *prosechein* – to watch, in the sense of looking intently. Perhaps it is not stretching language too far to see in this charge the call to the kind of contemplative watching I have been trying to describe.

If we are to perceive truth; if we are to discern the voice of the Holy Spirit; if our words are to become God's Word; if our ministry is to be transparent to Christ, then we must learn to become contemplatives.

Peter Nott is the Bishop of Norwich.

To Pray Always

ELIZABETH RUTH OBBARD ODC

I live in a Carmelite Monastery near Walsingham in Norfolk. From one side we can see the sea at Blakeney, from the other side we look out over rolling fields and pastureland. It is the sort of country which must have been dear to Julian, and our way of life imitates hers in some degree because it is based on continual prayer and seclusion. As enclosed nuns we don't go out to teach or nurse or visit; our apostolate is simply to *be* and to give witness to the love of Christ for all mankind through unceasing prayer. Nothing esoteric – just an ordinary day devoted to loving God, ordinary Christian life writ large and ordinary human life! Human because although each of us is a 'hermit' we do live in community and so get our fair share of family knocks and rubs!

The Rule we follow was first given to a group of hermits in thirteenth century Palestine and it has not lost its eremitical flavour. 'I chose Jesus for my heaven', said Julian. For her He was worth a lifetime of exclusive love and devotion: so it should be with us.

The day begins for a Carmelite at five-thirty, when we are awakened by a matraque (wooden rattle). That's the signal to leap up and begin a new day of prayer and praise. If left to myself, early rising would be very difficult but now I'm quite used to it and love the 'feel' of the dawn with its chorus of birds in the misty sky. Then it's down to Choir for Lauds, the morning office. After Lauds

we have a short break, then an hour of solitary prayer. Most of us like to spend this in our cells, or we can stay in Chapel or find a spot outside in fine weather. Solitary prayer is at the heart of our Carmelite life, a daily 'being with God', holding the whole world in our hearts and a desire to show the Lord He means more to us than anything else. In this silent waiting upon Him our life finds its meaning and its joy.

Then follows the Office of Terce, specially dedicated to the Holy spirit: 'May love light up our mortal frame 'til others catch the living flame.'

At eight o'clock we gather to cele- brate the Eucharist: this is our central act of worship at which we are nour- ished by the Bread of Life and listen together to God's Word.

Then we have a quick breakfast and repair to work. My goodness – so much time at prayer means getting a move on when it comes to earning

our living! We work in silence, and as far as possible alone:

vestment making

bookbinding

icon work

and all the various tasks needed in any family – cooking, gardening, cleaning . . . 'in all thing glorifying God.'

At 11.15 we meet for the Office of Sext and have a short period to examine our lives under God's gaze after which we go to dinner. We have a formal monastic refectory with a reader and server. As vegetarians we wish to share sym- bolically with the poor, but we have enough to eat, and we thank God for all we *do* have when so many are starving.

When dinner is over we all help with the washing-up and the preparation of the next day's vegetables, then it's back to work until 1.40.

1.45 – 2.45 signals a period of reading which is spent in the solitude of cell or garden. Although pride of place is obviously given to Scripture and

spiritual authors, we are encouraged to keep up a variety of cultural and intellectual interests – these keep us in touch with the wider world and enable us to enter more fully into the hopes and aspirations of all people. Reading is an essential element in a life of prayer for 'ignorance of the Scriptures is ignorance of Christ.'

At 2.45 we are in Choir for the Psalms of None, after which we return to work until 4.30 when we gather for Vespers. Before Vespers the novices of the community meet for a conference on some aspect of religious life. It's a life that needs a good foundation and, even after Solemn Vows, the nuns are expected to continue their studies and on-going formation.

Vespers is followed by another hour of silent prayer, then a frugal supper, usually of bread, cheese and fruit.

After supper we gather for an hour's recreation together, to share news, discuss, laugh and just rejoice in each other's company. Recreation gives

our hermit life a warm, sweet, family touch and, with no television or radio, we can offer each other our undivided attention. On special days we may play games or listen to recorded music and there is extra time together on big feasts, such as Christmas and Easter.

We go to Choir for the Office of Readings at 7.40. This takes about half an hour and includes not only psalms but two fairly substantial lessons, one from Scripture and the other from a spiritual writer.

Then we have free time – to write or draw, read or pray in the deep night silence when the whole house is quiet and each in her own cell. We gather for the last office at 9.30. Compline, the Church's night prayer, is gentle and meditative, sung to a guitar accompaniment.

And so to bed . . .
Not a *hard* life but a
demanding one; a life
which requires that
we be always 'there'
for God, listening to
His voice, and yet so
ordinary in many
aspects, an apostolate

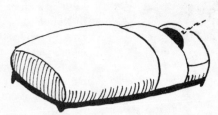

of being, not doing. Perhaps I could sum it up by sharing with you an extract of the prayer said over a nun at her Solemn Profession, and which each of you could use with some slight adaptation. 'Set her, Father, in the full radiance of the Face of Your Son, that she may catch His beauty, and by what she becomes show all the world that Jesus is living in His Church. Free from every selfish care may she take into herself the cares of her brethren, realising that in allaying the sorrows of others she is comforting the Lord Himself suffering in them. May the great human scene be lit up for her and given meaning by the vision of your providence at work always and everywhere. May the gift she makes of herself hasten the coming of Your Kingdom, and may she find her true place with all who love You in the Heavenly Fatherland, through Christ our Lord. Amen.'

Elizabeth Ruth Obbard ODC is Prioress of the Carmel of Walsingham in Langham, Norfolk. She is the author of several books on the spiritual life. The illustrations for this article are her own.

Teresa of Avila – Teacher of the Way of Prayer

ELIZABETH RUTH OBBARD ODC

I think we would have to go far to find any woman more vital, enthusiastic and gifted naturally and spiritually than St Teresa of Avila. In her we have a model of someone totally given to God and yet completely herself, with no hint of 'piosity', unnaturalness or a propensity to judge others. In fact, that last fault is one that she considered pernicious and an infallible indication that one had not even begun the real ascent to God, no matter how moral, prayerful and austere one's life might appear!

Teresa is both consolation and challenge for the one who wants to pray; consolation because she herself rose and fell many times as she so artlessly confesses; challenge because she is never satisfied until we have given God *everything* (though of course this is a progressive work, no one does it all at one fell swoop). 'Reflect – for this is the truth – God gives himself to those who give up everything for him' she wrote. If we are not prepared to take this attitude ourselves we are on the wrong path. But then she adds a rider, as always: if we can't match this resolution at least let's be honest and admit it 'for humility is the ointment for all our wounds'. Honesty is better than fine sentiments if we are to build *any* worthwhile relationship – with God or others.

All Teresa's teaching seems to revolve around this central activity and she speaks from her personal experience rather than from abstract principles – here differing from St John of the Cross, Carmel's other mystical doctor. Her preferred method of instruction is to use parables, metaphors and similes.

So prayer is like watering a garden – at first it takes of lot of effort and labour, later God himself waters the ground and we have little to do except receive what he is giving. The soul is like a precious jewel or a castle, at the centre of which dwells the King, whom we reach by travelling through a series of 'mansions'. We are like soft wax, ready to receive God's seal. We must act like the bee, busily gathering honey from many plants. Thus we can learn of Christ in many ways; better to concentrate on Him and His sweetness than upon ourselves. When we begin to be recollected at prayer God gives the ability to 'enter into ourselves' as if we were a hedgehog or tortoise. We are transformed into Christ as a tiny silk worm spins its cocoon and from whence emerges a beautiful butterfly . . .

All these examples flesh out Teresa's writing on prayer in which she conversationally and naturally shares her own experience of God's ways. Nowhere does she say that prayer will be easy, but she does insist that it is supremely worthwhile. Neither is Christianity 'easy' but it is worth everything we have. Jesus and the kingdom are the pearl of great price for which all else is bartered.

There is so much that could be said about Teresa as mistress of the spiritual life but here I would like to concentrate on what she has to say about the early stages. Later on, as she points out, God moves in and takes over. Our part is to make space for Him in prayer for, in her famous definition 'mental prayer, in my view, is nothing but friendly intercourse and frequent solitary converse with Him who we know loves us'.

First, a few preliminaries. Teresa cannot and does not divorce prayer from life. From her own experience she asserted that her life did not really begin until she began to pray. To pray is to enter into friendship with God (and especially Christ the God-Man) and friends want to be with each other, share their lives and concerns. Prayer as relationship will therefore be coloured by our various vocations and our natural temperament. Teresa was a very loving and sociable person, but she learned to develop a capacity for inwardness. Inwardness in her thoughts had nothing to do with introversion – which is something natural in a temperament – nor with introspection – which Teresa counselled people to avoid. Inwardness is about looking at God rather than ourselves, about loving *him*, pleasing *him*. 'Love does not consist in great sweetness of devotion but in a fervent determination to strive to please God in all things.' And we can know how our prayer is going, not by examining our inner feelings but our outward actions: 'We cannot know whether we love God, although there may be strong reasons for thinking so, but there can be no doubt about whether we love our neighbour. Be sure that in proportion as you advance in fraternal charity you are increasing in your love of God'.

If to pray is to enter into a relationship with God, it will grow and develop as does any relationship and perhaps in unexpected ways. Also, as time passes, we will have less to say and think about, be able to give more time to just loving. Teresa definitely counsels us not to spend all our prayer time thinking but to do whatever fosters the most love. 'Prayer consists not in thinking much but in loving much'.

So, how to begin? Teresa is a great comfort to those who find prayer hard. She admits that for twenty years she could not pray without having a book at hand, or a picture, anything to quieten her roving mind, give her something to support her. She never minimised the effort involved in learning to pray. We must find what suits our temperament and *work* at it, whether it be a Scriptural mantra, reflective reading, learning to 'look' at Jesus in silent love – her own preferred method – or praying by pondering/ praying the phrases of The Lord's Prayer as she describes so masterfully in her autobiographical *Way of Perfection*.

Other indispensible conditions are a pure conscience and the resolve to persevere and give God all he asks. There is no point in reaching a plateau and stopping, feeling we are good enough or perfect enough. We have to aim at total union with God. If we do our part, Teresa assures us, He will not fail on His part.

One thing Teresa does insist on. In prayer we can never neglect or 'get beyond' the human Christ. He is the Way. If we love Him, keep close to Him, we cannot go wrong from start to finish. Never can Jesus be dispensed with while we enter into a numinous cloud. He must be our Companion, our Lover, our Friend, our Bridegroom. 'With Him beside you you cannot err' she asserts.

A method Teresa encourages is to 'enter within' ourselves to look at Christ. I give it as an example of something practical but not to be slavishly followed. 'Do whatever helps you to love most', as she says.

St Teresa's Prayer of Recollection

Find a place where you can be quiet and still.

Collect your senses by means of observing nature or a picture, anything that will help you 'enter within' peacefully.

Make the sign of the cross, close your eyes. Simply try to quiet your soul and senses. This will prepare you to meet God.

Realise the presence of God within yourself by faith. Look at Jesus wordlessly and let Him look at you – either in one of His mysteries like the agony in the garden or just 'as He is'.

Heart to heart conversation: Let your heart speak. Let it say whatever it wants to, honestly. Simply share your thoughts and feelings with the Lord.

Then rest silently in His love.

I would emphasise that this is only *one* method, others may help you more – such as the slow recitation of a vocal prayer. Whatever you choose, persevere and don't be afraid of labour or dryness. With time, if we do what we can, God will take over, draw us into His own life and love. Our part, as a tiny silkworm, is to spin the cocoon – pray, read Scripture, grow in love for others, selflessness, attention to daily duties. Then, when we have done all *we* can we shall be 'hidden' with Christ in God', taken into the dark cocoon from which we will, in God's good time, emerge as a butterfly, free, beautiful and ready for the new life and union which only He can give us.

Silence

GERVASE O'DONOHOE

Silence is listening. It is allowing oneself to be receptive. So much of the noise we seek out and the noise we encourage within ourselves is simply a way of keeping other people's real concerns at bay. Silence is a way of being open to reality and to truth, and in our anxiety to avoid the truth about ourselves or about a situation we can become great escapists from silence. It is a phenomenon that we all know too well. There is a sort of Tower of Babel within each one of us, and the Babel story in Genesis is, of course, a 'fall' story. Our dislike of silence, our unwillingness to listen to ourselves or to others, is a part of our fallen nature. We are afraid, foolishly, of what we might hear.

Silence is a journey inward because the first and most insistent thing that we become aware of in silence is ourselves. It is, indeed, our self that first reduces us to silence, because, although we can hold the world and our fellow men's concerns at bay by seeking out noise, we cannot entirely blot out our consciousness of our selves and the insistent questions that the mystery of our own being puts to us. Human beings have always been aware that they cannot escape from themselves.

The first effect of silence, therefore, is to make us aware of the Babel of conflicting desires that are alive within us, and so it demands that we make some sense of them and give them some direction. In fact, it is the desire for direction, for a sense of perspective, that awakens the longing for silence. We experience the need to come to terms with all that noise inside us. What does it all mean? What is it telling us? How much of it is real and sound? How much illusory? St Gregory the Great recognised that it was in silence that our real desire was revealed when he wrote: 'For it is not our words that make the stronger impression on the ears of God, but our desires. Thus, if we seek eternal life with the mouth, but do not really desire it with the heart, when we cry out we are really silent. But if we desire in the heart, even when our mouth is silent, in our silence we cry aloud.'

Silence is a self-emptying, too, because to come to single-mindedness in all our purposes demands opening ourselves to what is the origin, centre and end of all our being – the other, God. To achieve this we have to leave ourselves behind, and while the noise is on we are in control. Once the noise is silenced, that which is real, true, there, and insistent, takes over. We control our lives by means of our rational processes; and a great part of our self-emptying when we enter into silence is 'the folding of the wings of the intellect to open the door of the heart', as Catherine Doherty puts it in *Poustinia*. This is the object for those who seek God who, as the author of *The Cloud of Unknowing* reminds us, can be caught and held by love but by thinking never. Perhaps, most clearly, silence is a self-emptying for us because we use noise to bolster our illusions about ourselves, or to enable us to live, seemingly, on several levels at once – all confused, with the establishing of priorities put off until another day. Christianity understands that a person who avoids silence eludes himself or herself and eludes God too.

Silence is not an escape from reality, even when we take a few days away from it all in search of it. The rather glib modern assumption that it is an escape presupposes that the noise and bustle of life is the 'real' world, and not, as so often, simply a cover for a loss of sense of direction. We may need some time in physical retirement from our everyday round to come to terms with reality, but the silence that we are talking about here is, in the end, a silence within our own hearts. It is an attentive, listening attitude to life. What this silence brings, then, is not a detachment from life and all its activities, but an attachment to something greater so that we can move through life's rush and still keep all things in a right perspective.

A striking example of what this means is the attitude of Jesus in all the events surrounding the death of Lazarus (John 11). Jesus moves through all the rush and panic and tears stirred up by this death with a calm assurance which is based on his firm hold on something greater – his certain trust that the Father will hear his prayer. But he is not detached. Quite the opposite, he is completely involved, and weeps.

One other most important fruit of silence is the retention of a sense of wonder which comes from a true awareness of reality and its mystery. This wonder is, in the end, a wonder at God's presence. God it is who is the still centre of our being. He makes himself known in this silence. He is the direction which we need to sense. He is the something greater to which we need to be attached so as to counteract the forces in our lives which would tend to pull us apart. It is in him that all the warring factions of our desires can come to the peace table. He is the one who reveals to us our real selves – his image within us, which asks the nagging questions that invite us into the silence in which the glorious answer is experienced.

Gervase O'Donohoe teaches religion at St Peter's School, Guildford.

A Feather in the Early Morning
URSULA PARRY

I was woken early one morning by peals of laughter, giggles, squeals and sounds of real joy. It immediately made me feel good tempered and also naturally curious, as my usual dawn chorus is of disagreement and calls for adjudication because things 'aren't fair'. It turned out to be two of my children, Benedict, then aged nine, and three-year-old Alice playing with nothing more than a small feather. They were throwing it up in the air and trying to catch it before it fell to the ground or on to the bed below. 'Look', said Benedict, 'Alice is really good at it.' And she was, because she was patiently waiting for the feather to fall into her open hands, instead of snatching at it, which would have caused currents of air to whoosh the feather unexpectedly from its path of descent. But this very unpredictability was the cause of the mirth and squeals of delight, and they added to the game by puffs of breath especially when it was the other's turn to do the catching.

All this led me to reflect on Hildegard of Bingen and how she sees herself as a 'feather on the breath of God'. I can imagine God could be as joyful as my children were, as he gently blows us on his breath, delighting in the pure goodness of his creation. Here are Hildegard's words about the Holy Spirit:

> 'The Holy Spirit is life that gives life,
> Moving all things.
> It is the root in every creature
> And purifies all things,
> Wiping away sins,
> Anointing wounds.
> It is radiant life, worthy of praise,
> Awakening and enlivening
> All things.'

Then I thought that the breath of God is not like the fickle child's breath, teasing his sister with unexpected puffs, but sure and utterly to be relied upon. Again Hildegard's words from *The Book of Divine Works* - visions where she heard a voice speaking to her:

> 'I, the highest and fiery power, have kindled every living spark and I have breathed out no thing that can die ... And by means of the airy wind, I stir everything into quickness with a certain invisible life which sustains all.'

It also occurred to me that we must make ourselves light and free like a feather and trust completely to this joyful God who blows us onwards but is always there to catch us in his sure open hands. Hildegard suffered chronic ill health later in her life and this is what she says in one of her letters:

> 'But in these two respects - in my body and my soul - I do not know myself and reckon myself as nothing and rely on the living God and I leave all these things to him, so that he who has no beginning and no end may in all these things, keep me safe from evil.'

The joy of God, the sureness and the need for us to surrender to his gentle breath - not bad for a few joyful moments in the morning, but as Hildegard says in the last words of her *Scivias*:

> 'Let the one who has ears sharp enough to hear inner meanings ardently love My reflection and pant after My words and inscribe them in his soul and conscience. Amen.'

The Abbey of Bec Hellouin

URSULA PARRY

This community of monks dates from 1060, when Herluin, who was formerly a Norman knight founded it in the beautiful valley of Bec, near Brionne in Normandy. Under his successor Anselm the abbey became an influential centre of Anglo-Norman Christianity and learning. Three Archbishops of Canterbury (Lanfranc, Anselm and Theobald), three Bishops of Rochester, and seven abbots of English communities came from the Bec Hellouin. Much of the abbey was destroyed during the Hundred Years' War and was rebuilt during the seventeenth century.

In 1948 Benedictine monks were invited to return to the abbey and they restored it. At about the same time the Moniales of Sainte Francoise Romaine moved from Paris to the valley of Bec, two miles from the abbey. The foundress of this order was a widow in the fifteenth century who, after a happy married life, wanted to live as happy a religious life in community as she had lived with her husband. So her order was linked with the Olivetan Monks of St Maria Novella. The two communities follow in this tradition today, uniting for some of the services and making decisions jointly. They seem to regard each other as equals, and the sisters are by no means subservient to the brothers.

Visitors are received by the sisters who, although living a life of contemplative prayer, offer hospitality according to the Rule of St Benedict: 'Let all guests be received like Christ'. They have several guest houses, including a barn where large groups can stay, and from several of the rooms you can hear the peaceful murmuring of the Bec. They are very welcoming to English visitors because of ties between Bec and Canterbury, and it seems to be a tradition that the Archbishops of Canterbury pay a visit to Bec.

The sisters have their own small chapel at their monastery, but on Sundays and feast days they travel the two miles down to the abbey by bus. There they join with the monks in singing the services in a most beautiful way. The chapel at the abbey was originally the dining hall, but was used by Napoleon to stable his horses during the Revolution. After Mass in the morning, the monks give guided tours of the abbey, and several of the original features can be seen, including the tower of the church and the cloisters.

It is very difficult to convey how special a place Bec is. It is certainly one of those places where 'prayer has been valid'; time seems to stand still; and it gives one great confidence to see the sisters and brothers just content 'to be' – in their daily lives. Here is a quotation from St Anselm's which seems to describe what happens there.

> Come frail man! It is time to flee for a while your daily occupations. Divest yourself this once of the tumult of your thoughts, reject now the worries that weigh you down and put off your workaday concerns. Consecrate to God, be it only in a meagre part, your activity, and rest in Him. Descend into the secrecy of your soul and banish from it all save God and that which leads to Him. Then, the door firmly closed, seek Him out. O my heart, say keeping nothing back, say unto God: 'I seek Thy face, it is Thy face O Lord that I desire. (Psalm 26).
> *Proslogion*, St Anslem, Abbott at the Bec Hellouin, 1078–1092

Taizé: Where Melody and Silence Meet

URSULA PARRY

Taizé is a small village in Burgundy in Southern France near Cluny and Lyons. It is a place of prayer and pilgrimage for people of all ages, though the majority are 15–30. They come from all over the world to take part in the week-long meetings and join in the prayer of the community. But the community of men grew from very small beginnings. It was started by Brother Roger, who is the Prior of Taizé today, who used his home as a place to welcome refugees during the war and then gradually men came who wanted to share in his life. These were not just people from his Lutheran Church, but from all denominations and backgrounds, so Taizé now is an ecumenical community.

There is a large community of brothers living at Taizé, as well as small groups of them living in some of the poorest parts of the world. They welcome several thousands of people every week. The basis of these week-long meetings is the prayer of the community, which has three services in the church every day. These services are very beautiful. They contain all the elements one would expect: intercession, readings, psalms and singing but, because of the many languages represented, everything has to be very simple, with few words and these are translated into several languages. After the main reading, usually there is a long silence, about 15 minutes, which has a great depth to it considering there could be several thousands of people in church. I think the secret of this unity of spirit is the fact that silence and music are languages that can be understood by everyone.

The week culminates in the weekend which re-enacts the events of Good Friday through to Easter Day. On Friday morning there is veneration of the cross and use of orthodox music. At the end of the service, those who wish, lay their foreheads on the cross to identify with the suffering of Christ in his world. On Saturday evening there is the service of light where all the people have a candle which is lit for the gospel. At the end of these services, people often pray for several hours in the church and sometimes all night. On Sunday morning there is a Eucharist, after which most of the groups pack up and go home. The music for these last three services is extra special, as a small group of musicians will have been practising during the week, both singers and instrumentalists.

In between the services the time is normally spent in discussion groups, especially on your first visit, but it is also possible to spend the week in silence, in a special place set aside for that, or to work in the café or in welcoming people, or doing jobs around Taizé. Every afternoon there is a singing practice and there are also meetings during the week to meet other people from your own country. To spend a week in Taizé is to encounter both yourself as you really are and the reality of God: you always seem to have been changed in some way and come back with a new way of looking at life and a broader understanding of the Church.

The accommodation is fairly basic for the younger people, either in tents or in sheds with bunk beds and mattresses. For the older people and families who go, there is more comfortable accommodation but you need to book well in advance to be sure of a place. I would recommend Taizé as a place for families; there is a special place set aside for them, and people are organised to look after the children during the discussions. The children also have their own sessions and a service in the afternoon.

The community publishes a bi-monthly *Letter from Taizé*, which has an article usually by Brother Roger and readings for each day, which are those used at the services in Taizé. There are also several books by Brother Roger which I have found useful for 'lead-ins', most of which are published by Mowbrays in London.

For further information about staying at Taizé, write to the Taizé Community, Taizé, Cluny 71250, France.

Ursula Parry is a violinist, teacher and the mother of three children. She is married to a vicar in the Witney Team Ministry.

Contrary States

D. J. PASKINS

> Small talk in urgency
> Fills the room
> With the throng
> And its song
> Of indolence and of expediency.
>
> Silence of ecstasy
> Stills the wood,
> And the trees
> Hold their peace
> Of innocence and of expectancy.

D. J. Paskins is Rector of Bere Ferrers with Bere Alston, Devon.

Christian and Buddhist

JOHN RICHARDS

From their very origins Christianity and Buddhism have had a great difference of ethos and emphasis. Buddhism was primarily a monastic religion.
Some would say it still is. Christianity on the other hand was primarily a
lay religion, and even today monasticism sometimes has to justify itself.
Not unrelatedly, Buddhism was ruthlessly unsymbolic, undescriptive,
unspeculative. For all its clarity and practical emphasis there is a certain
bleakness about it, particularly in its early form, that contrasts with the
rich, and at times perhaps opaque, symbolism and imagery that Christianity
owes to its biblical, semitic background. Moreover, partly because of its
very clarity, Buddhism, while extremely tolerant, does not seem to have
the capacity of Christianity to assimilate highly diverse traditions, though
the history of Buddhism in China may indicate that it is not necessarily
the case.

Previous generations tended to see an unbridgeable divide between the
'theistic' faith of Christianity and the 'atheistic' approach of Buddhism.
More recent writers, however, like Thomas Merton and Aelred Graham on
the one side and Buddhadasa on the other, have rightly seen that although
this difference of expression will affect the ethos, it is not so fundamental
as it looks at first sight. When God is not merely *a* Being, however exalted,
but Being, or the 'Ground' of Being itself, then the 'personal' aspect of
God is but a manner of speaking – the Christian affirmation, as Dean Inge
used to say, that in prayer the Christian is not just soliloquising. Similarly
it is now more widely recognised that even if Buddhism does not use any
term comparable to 'God' for its ultimate reality and aim, it clearly has *got*
an absolute and transcendent aim, and a very positive affirmation of it.

At the same time the emphasis on 'practice', in the sense of meditation,
is far more consistent and explicit in Buddhism than in Christianity where
exhortations to prayer in the Bible, even the New Testament, are fairly
general and not obviously focal, as meditation clearly is in Buddhism, where
it constitutes the culminating last two steps of the Buddhist 'Noble Eightfold
Path'. What is perhaps surprising in view of this emphasis, and in spite of
a significant revival in recent years, is how few Buddhist monks do in fact
meditate at all in indigenously Buddhist countries.

The Westerner often gets the idealised impression that every Buddhist
monastery is filled with saffron-clad monks wrapped in *Samadhi* or deep
contemplation. But as a westerner who spent several years in various
countries in the East, as a Buddhist monk, I must testify that this is sadly
just not so. Would to God that it were. Yet what there is, is often of a
surprisingly high quality.

Even now, as a Christian priest, I look back on my training in Buddhist meditation as one of the most demanding and valuable experiences of my life. For days, usually weeks on end, under the careful and daily guidance of his teacher, the pupil spends not just an hour or two, but *the whole day*, and every day, alternately sitting in meditation (usually for an hour at a time) and then walking up and down, also in meditation. In the one case his main focus of attention will be on his breathing, in the latter on the movement of the legs in walking.

The essential principle is very simple – that as the mind becomes progressively more still by the avoidance of emotive distraction, he sees things more and more clearly, until eventually he will see things 'as they truly are', in the Buddhist phrase, which is indeed one expression of the whole aim of the Buddhist life. That meditation can in any ultimate sense lead to 'seeing things as they truly are' must in a sense be an article of faith originally. But few people, I think, who have done more than just dabble in meditation have any fundamental reservation about the claim.

While Buddhist meditation is in its main forms ruthlessly nonconceptual and completely focussed on the present moment, the main stream of Christian spirituality has flowed in rather different channels. There has been an 'apophatic' (*Via Negativa*) tradition in Christianity as well, of course, particularly in the Eastern Church. It probably owed its origins more to Platonic than to biblical sources, but we tend to forget nowadays how almost completely platonised the Church was at one time. The tradition exemplified and spread under the name of the great Dionysius the Areopagite is certainly more Greek than Semitic . . .

'In your intent practice of mystical contemplation, abandon both the senses and the intellectual faculties – and all the objects of senses and intellect, and all things with or without being, and reach in unknowing up to the unity of that which is above all being and knowledge.'

Early baptised, this tradition has had a long run and is still by no means done, as the high esteem in which *The Cloud of Unknowing* is held testifies. The similarity of this tradition to Buddhist practices is evident, and those drawn to it may well find inspiration, clarification and technical assistance from Buddhist sources, just as early Christians did from Platonic ones.

Yet this has not been the main stream of Christian spirituality. The main stream of Christian spirituality has been devotional. Through *Lectio Divina*, the devout, contemplative browsing in the Bible and other classics, and the loving meditation (thought) about the actions and words of Our Lord, the typical Christian contemplative has learned to arouse and develop love. (Book 3, Chapter 5 of Thomas à Kempis' *The Imitation of Christ* gives a fine picture of this.) For this sort of practice the rich, symbolic language of biblical thought is well equipped. The modern critical spirit, however, has made this use of the Bible less easy than it used to be, and the same must be said for modern theology, which is largely anti-allegorical and anti-mystical. But is even this devotional approach so radically different from the precise Buddhist practice of watching the breathing? In practice, I think not. In practice, as the scriptures attest, the great turning point in Buddhist meditation is the arising of *joy*. This stabilises and satisfies the mind which up to its coming is restless and dissatisfied. In the classic Buddhist practice joy arises spontaneously, unsought. It seems to be a sort of overflow of energy no longer being dissipated in emotive thought and nervous tension. Some Buddhist practices like the meditation on 'Loving Kindness' (Metta) actively induce it. The difference, however, between Love and Joy seems to me an academic one. It is essentially that the one has an object while the other has not. The effect on the mind is the same. It is now deeply satisfied and at last prepared to be still, leaving lesser things behind forgotten and unhankered after.

The Christian has one obstacle which, by and large, the Buddhist does not, though it is less widespread than it used to be. After the 'Quietist Controversy' of the eighteenth century, to stop actively thinking in prayer tended to be discouraged in the West, forgetting that the thinking was really only a stepping stone to the arousal of love. But one temptation the Christian and the Buddhist both share. There is a natural inclination to cling to the pleasure of love or joy, and to the sense of success that it gives. But both need to learn to go beyond the consciously emotive and satisfying love or joy to a deeper peace and quiet waiting for what 'eye has not seen, nor ear heard, and what has not arisen in the mind of man'.

As Teresa of Avila used to say, too many people stop praying (and meditating) just when it is really becoming prayer.

John Richards is a parish priest in the Anglican tradition, and was for ten years a Buddhist monk and meditation instructor. He tells us that he likes the label for himself, if label there must be, of 'Anglo-Catholic', understanding thereby 'English and completely universalist'.

Meditation and Healing

DIANA ROANTREE

I want to explore something of the relationship between meditation and healing. By the term meditation I mean non-discursive meditation. I choose this word rather than contemplation because I am not confining myself to religious meditation. I believe that non-religious or secular meditation and religious meditation are physiologically the same. Both are concerned to penetrate beyond the rational wordy consciousness of everyday to a deeper and unifying consciousness. 'What makes meditation religious or non-religious is one's sense of values and one's motivation,' says William Johnston in his book *Silent Music*.

Recent research in the field of consciousness identifies four principal brainwaves. Of these delta is the slow rhythm found in deep sleep and theta is associated with drowsiness, while alpha and beta occur normally in consciousness. Beta is the high-frequency brainwave most common in our waking hours. Alpha is slower and more reflective. Most people begin to produce alpha when they close their eyes and relax.

It is the alpha rhythm that is of particular interest. Experiments show that people who meditate move easily into alpha. 'Physiologically speaking (the meditative state) seems to be characterised by high-amplitude alpha brainwaves.' As Johnston also remarks:

> One can understand why the old spiritual masters discouraged conceptualization and discursive thinking in time of contemplation. What they were discouraging was the focused awareness or the superficial visualization which characterises conceptual thought. This . . . blocks alpha and brings one into beta, thus destroying the conditions most favourable to contemplative experience. Put in scientific terms, what the spiritual masters wanted was to bring their disciples into an alpha state and keep them there.

That is a point well worth pondering by anyone involved in the Julian Meetings, although somewhat aside from the present discussion.

It was a Radio 4 programme entitled 'Would You Go To A Healer?' that set me thinking about meditation and healing. In the programme Maxwell Cade described his experiments to find out if there is a connection between healing and levels of consciousness. In addition to the four principal levels he spoke of a 'State Five . . . in which you can carry the calmness of meditation with you in everyday life'. Few people showed State Five brainwave patterns when Cade made his first experiments, but:

> 'Later, when we measured our first healer, we were surprised to find immediately that that was the pattern the healer was showing. Later we found that she didn't show it normally but only when she was healing or thinking about healing. The next thing which we found at the very same session was that she induced this pattern in her patients, and this seems to be the real mark of the healer – the ability to induce in their patients a particular brainwave pattern which seems to be associated with an acceleration of the body's natural healing processes.'

I see a partial link here with the meditation movement exemplified in Transcendental Meditation. This is positively therapeutic in purpose. Scientifically speaking, the aim is to generate high-amplitude alpha as an antidote to the divisive pressures of a technological age. In this instance self-help, not at the hands of a healer. And of mind more than body. But employing the same power? I think so. Which brings us to the question of how healing works.

Like other healers, Bruce Macmanaway, also featured in the Radio 4 programme, finds 'deep relaxation and meditation' important. In meditation a person relaxes from active discursive participation (beta state) passively to produce slower speed and higher voltage alpha brainwaves. A lot of *passive energy* is generated. In TM – and indeed in Christian contemplation, although this is but one aspect of that story – the meditator is stilled and rested and restored, and maybe carries a little of his calm with him into the workaday world.

In healing, the picture is rather more complex. The 'great air of stillness' which Cade finds characterises all the effective healers points clearly to the presence of high-amplitude alpha (in State Five). Is it also that through the healer passive energy is channeled to others so that his patients, not unlike the meditator, can relax and be healed? It would be foolish to dogmatise, but I am disposed to see it this way. And disposed, too, to find in the concept of passive energy generated in meditation a rational approach in answer to those who dismiss contemplative prayer as a waste of time. But this is another topic.

After seventeen years in teacher training, Diana Roantree worked for nine years with the Open University in East Anglia. Now retired, she lives in Dorset.

Be Opened!

DAVID SELF

> On his journey back from Tyrian territory he went by way of Sidon to the sea of Galilee, well within the territory of the Decapolis. They brought to him a man who was deaf and had an impediment in his speech, and begged Jesus to lay his hands on him. He took him aside, away from the crowd; then he put his fingers in the man's ears, and touched his tongue with spittle. Looking up to heaven, he sighed, and said to him, 'Ephphatha,' which means 'Be opened.' With that his hearing was restored, and at the same time the impediment was removed and he spoke clearly. Jesus forbade them to tell anyone; but the more he forbade them, the more they spread it abroad. Their astonishment knew no bounds: 'All that he does, he does well,' they said; 'he even makes the deaf hear and the dumb speak.' (Mark 7:31–37)

Healthy babies are born with their senses functioning acutely, but the impressions they receive are totally disorganised. They have to learn slowly how to organise all the impressions they are receiving in order even to begin to make sense of their new world – responding to the mother's touch, the father's voice, the smell of the breast, and so on. There are so many impressions coming in that soon, very soon, the child must learn how to select, and therefore how *not* to hear or see or feel. Our capacity to do this gradually increases and hardens without our noticing, like a gradual deafness, as we learn how to cope and survive in a world which inexplicably hurts. We learn how to protect ourselves. The barriers grow more rigid, we lose resilience as we grow older and we carry more and more baggage of unresolved life from the past. We learn how not to live, developing tramline patterns of thought and behaviour, increasing the noise and activities around us to drown the silence within. Because the silence might mean death – or even worse, emptiness. And so our deadness spreads and we think it's normal.

Perhaps one picture of the church is that of the deaf-mute being brought to Jesus. Here we are, being taken aside, close to our Lord. Here we are, dulled in senses, with a bar across the door, unable to share easily that which is in the heart, waiting to be touched by his Spirit as he sighs to the Father. Be opened, be released, become alive! Jesus, the most alive of all human beings, fully rooted in his Father, the source of all life, came to share his aliveness. People recognised not only his vitality but also his connection with the Father and his capacity to release people into new life. And they drew near in their muteness, paralysis and disease. Here was one who by his teaching, praying and healing could say with authority:

> Be opened in your hearts.
> Let your minds be released into new
> understanding
> Let the senses of your body unfurl to
> all that is around you.
> Become alive.

And it hurts! Who said that healing wouldn't hurt? God sets before us life and death. Choose life – choose to remain vulnerable, with all the pain that being alive entails, so that you go on being open and responsive all through your life. Jesus would say to us; Be open, be channels of the life-giving, reviving power of the risen Christ. We cannot enjoy life privately, for to be alive is to be aware of those around us and hold them before the dynamic flowing love of God in our prayers and living. I have in mind two specific examples.

First, everything we do has a mixture of motives – some good, some not so good. We can be very good at carping, criticising destructively, sniffing out the bad motives. Perhaps we could do something positive; like looking for what is good in other people, and when we find something good, genuinely appreciate it and tell them. Nothing unbars the door faster than an unexpected gift of appreciation and praise. It would be so good and life-sharing if the Church could be known as a place where people are naturally encouraged, where goodness is discerned and God is praised by it!

Secondly, the hardest lesson St Paul had to learn was that much of his ministry came through his weakness, not his strength. Our strengths are God-given, and it is right that we develop and use them in God's service with a profound sense of thanksgiving. But they too easily become sources of pride, used against others rather than for them. It takes a lot longer to learn that our weaknesses are also God-given, and to be accepted as an important part of our identity through which God has a special access to our souls. Christ has entered into our condition so that we could draw near in our muteness. He does not take away our weaknesses but he does give us the courage to go on being opened and vulnerable there. Through the wounds and fragilities that we all carry, the grace of God draws near to touch the core of our beings and flow out from us to others.

I now give you a symbol, a rope with knots in it, to represent your life. Take a nylon rope and let the Spirit take you through the memories of your life. If the rope represents your life, then begin slowly at one end and make a knot in it every time your memory calls up a significant event or person around which are clustered considerable feelings. Begin with your earliest memories and move slowly to the present. Once you have the knotted rope, go back and hold a particular knot of your life before our Lord, without analyzing it or saying much about it, but praying in your muteness for his transforming touch. You can do this with as many knots as you wish over a period of time. The knotted rope can also act as a kind of personal rosary, whereby you can praise God for the grace that has come to you and through you at the points of your fragility.

The power of transformation is the love of God brought to us in Christ. He has changed our whole vision of God and made it possible to draw near. We are bonded to him through the love his Spirit brings to our spirits. By saying, 'Yes', to our baptism, we say, 'Yes', to the Spirit preparing us for the eternal dance of love in the Trinity. Opening ourselves to contemplation is to open ourselves to the dynamic flow of God praying through us. We experience God as Trinity.

We speak of God as Father, Son and Holy Spirit. These are word-pictures of relationships. God is not a divine solitariness, a divine aloof egotism. Nor is God a committee of independent beings, as if one showed Isaiah a vision, another came along in Jesus, and a third appear as the Spirit. We experience God as Trinity, through glimpsing the way God is working to create and to make us whole. The bonding of the three persons of the Trinity is a bond of love so deep that to meet one is to meet all three in that One. We look at Jesus, and we see the Father (as he tells Philip) and encounter the Spirit of Jesus. Through the Spirit, Jesus points us to the one he teaches us to call, 'Father'. The Father says to us, 'Here is my Son, my Beloved', and the Spirit of God whom Jesus gives us teaches us of the deep things of God.

We look to the Triune God, that daring, dancing Trinity, that perfect Communion where love is constantly exchanged. Can we say anything about all that? Perhaps we can. Since the Triune God is our creator, the likeness of his eternal, dynamic loving dwells in the human race. The

Trinity in Unity is the source of human fellowship in those who repent of their self-centred isolation and discover the true principle of their being. Being still before God is to desire the love of the Trinity to flow through us in prayer. Much silent prayer is an attempt to give God permission to do just that - asking the Spirit to pray through our spirits as he joins us to Christ who holds the world and us in prayer as he cries, 'Abba, Father'.

What are the qualities of God-loving? In his book *God and Man* (DLT, 1979) Metropolitan Anthony of Sourozh reminds us that when we think of loving, we think of giving and receiving. And these are important elements, especially when they are purified and become means of committing ourselves in expressions of service, of worship, of tenderness, of the humility of a generous heart. That applies to both giving and receiving. If a person is always just giving, or just receiving, that is not love because one is dominating the other. When there is both giving and receiving, is that enough? No, because the relationship remains unstable. There needs to be a third quality, that of stepping aside, the ability to accept not to be.

'By this I mean the following; John the Baptist said about himself, "I am the friend of the Bridegroom". The bride is not his bride, neither is the bridegroom his bridegroom, but such is his love for them both that he brings them together - he is their witness and their companion in the marriage feast; he brings them to the chamber where they will meet face to face alone in a fulfilled relationship of soul and body, and he remains outside, lying across the door, so that no one should disturb the mystery of this love. This act of self-annihilation is essential to love, and if there is no such thing in our love, with regard not only to one person but to all persons, all situations, all things, our love is still deficient. This is very important for us to understand because in God we find the three things. We find the exulting joy of three persons who love in giving perfectly and receiving perfectly, but who, being a trinitarian relationship, if I may put it in this form of speech, are not in the way of each other. Each of them accepts, at every single moment, not to exist for the other two who are face to face - the miracle of total communion, fusion and one-ness.'

So we in silence offer ourselves to God. We are open to receive from God whatever he would give us, but we would desire to lay ourselves aside for God, so that the Spirit of Christ will pray through our spirits to the Father. Giving, receiving, creating space for others to be truly themselves. These are the elements of loving which reflect the eternal dance of the Trinity, where love is in constant delighted exchange, and into which we are called to become truly human together.

David Self is Rector of the Dunstable Team Ministry and has a long standing association with Julian Meetings.

Candlemas: A Meditation

DAVID SINGLETON

Outside
the aromatic light,
warm to the tongue;

but these are dark doors
and walls ten ages deep.

The pilgrim flame who enters here
outgrows his frame
or disappears;
sears shape and plane, burns blind his shine,
rebrands his name,
or falls to time.

For these are dark doors,
the walls ten ages deep.

God grant
the pilgrim lantern
fire.

Secret Tradition

DAVID SINGLETON

They say
in the high caverns
the light is crystal-dark,
the darkness light as air.

They say
the clouds up there
hide all and nothing,
singing silent secrets.

They say
on that mountain
clambering souls grow careless,
fall to their death
and live.

Poem

DAVID SINGLETON

> Find me
> when a mischief fails
> when solitary seconds
> winning the hour
> web the world with windows.
>
> Follow
> down the still descent
> to cavernous repose
> where every dream
> and three false dawns
> postpone first light
> invincible.
>
> Know me
> as your worded thoughts
> disperse in fire
> and die.

David Singleton is Senior Lecturer in Applied Linguistics at Trinity College, Dublin, and Secretary General of the Association Internationale de Linguistique Appliquée. His poems printed here 'represent the outpourings of a research student in his twenties'.

Soul Polishing

KENNEDY THOM

In a church where I was once a curate, we had a very pious server. During the Eucharist he would sometimes take off into an ecstasy of private devotion that prevented him from carrying out his duties. The rector used to get very irritated. 'Walter's soul polishing again' he would snort.

Soul polishing is an accusation that is sometimes made of those trying to practise contemplative prayer. Public worship, the prayer of intercession and even meditation are seen to have some point, in that they all have direct bearing on the praying person's relationships with other people. Hence they fall within the general category of loving others. But contemplative prayer – sitting still, thinking about nothing, often alone – while it may be good as a personal relaxation technique, does not, according to these critics, pass the test of Christian concern for the neighbour.

Such criticism is justified where contemplative prayer is allowed to become an end in itself. The discipline of prayer is not a matter of developing techniques to get what you want. Contemplative love can never be for something which one jealously guards from contamination, taking it out to play with at set prayer times. As long as we see contemplative love as a thing to be acquired, we shall be tempted to build walls round it for its safe keeping. Then our critics will be justified in their accusations of selfishness and soul polishing.

Rather the true discipline of prayer means the realising of a solitude in which we learn not to seek love but to give it. Our contemplative love is not for some *thing* but towards some *one*, who so far from being held in by our prayer, can and does break out on the world. Contemplation thus becomes an instrument for making our faith portable, for following the One we love into the world, there to apprehend the reality of God's presence and action. As Alan Ecclestone puts it, 'Contemplative living is really a matter of learning to see'. What we see and respond to is a God whose ways are not our ways, who is from our point of view completely unpredictable. Without the transcending of all images, which is the way of contemplation, we shall be unable to listen to and perceive this unpredictability. We shall still be stuck with the idols of our own fantasy, first among which is the importance of our thoughts about God and our concern for His business.

' "Be still and know that *I* am God" ... Too often we do not picture prayer in the way God invites us here; we think of it as a terribly important, serious thing that we have to do, mentally lining it up with all the other important things that pile up on our desks, those weighty matters that depend on us and require our urgent attention. But God is inviting us to take a break, to play truant. We can stop doing all those things we have to do in our capacity as God and leave it to Him to be God' (Simon Tugwell, in *Prayer*).

We have to abandon for ever the idea, all too prevalent among us, that we can make God come to us in prayer. We delude ourselves that by setting apart certain times and places for prayer and by devoting our attention to God, we shall somehow tempt him nearer and get to know him better, as if he were like a shy robin and we possessed of a plate of crumbs. He is there at every moment of every day: in our waking, our sleeping, our living and working, God is. Contemplative prayer helps us to discern Him better, to see Him in our world and to respond to what He is doing. Abhishiktananda writes, 'To live in prayer is to live in the presence of God'. Here too we have a clue to what St Paul meant when he encouraged the Thessalonians to 'pray without ceasing' (I Thess. 4:17).

The end which the Christian has to serve is not his own spiritual satisfaction, but the consecration of all life to God by the leaven of holiness and hence by the spiritual vitality of the members of the body of Christ. The tension is not between the sacred and the profane, between my prayer time and my daily routine, but between a world turned in on itself and a world that is in the process of becoming. In the latter we are co-creators with God, in as far as we are able to discern Him at work and to give ourselves to forwarding the growth and sanctification of human beings, to help them reach up to the fullness of the stature of Christ. As Thomas Merton puts it, 'What is important today is not to get man to accept religion as a human or cultural value, but to let him see that we are witnesses of Christ, of the new creation, of the Resurrection; that goes far beyond the phenomenon of religion'.

Seen from this perspective, contemplative prayer is the fundamental factor in the discerning and consequent advancing of God's work of redemption and sanctification in the world. This poem by A. K. Clarke, 'The Raising of Lazarus' – expresses what that means both for the one who prays and for the dead world which Christ in His own Resurrection calls into new life.

> Not by an instant's magic, overthrowing
> All nature's laws of building and decay,
> But by the mystery of power inflowing
> From those two days of silence far away
> He gave the kiss of life to Lazarus,
> Drawing him gently to his resurrection.
>
> Silence and peace, restoring us each day,
> Releasing our true selves without our knowing
> And drawing each towards his own perfection, –
> Here is the touch of heaven for each of us,
> These are the laws which guide our spirit's growing.

Kennedy Thom is Chaplain at the Christian Centre for Medical and Spiritual Care, Burrswood.

Little Gidding

ANN TILLEY

To live in a place 'where prayer has been valid' for three hundred years makes challenges. The peace of the countryside may lead to a misunder-standing of what it means to live in this Cambridgeshire hamlet. But the vigour of the wind which blows up from the Alconbury brook to the Manor Farm gives some inkling of the way in which the life of the community has to be open to the Spirit.

We twenty-five or so, adults and children, who live here today, inherit a tradition of worship and service to the immediately locality. In the seven-teenth century the Ferrar family busied themselves with education, with the Harmonies of the Gospels, with a dispensary, with bookbinding and the housekeeping and homemaking of a large extended family. Children were important (Nicholas's sister Susannah Collett had sixteen) and three school-masters taught the younger members of the family and sundry cousins. On Sundays the local children, who had learnt their Psalms, came to be tested by Nicholas Ferrar's elder nieces. The children were rewarded with a good Sunday lunch and a penny for each Psalm correctly recited. The Ferrar family had thus initiated what was probably the first Sunday School. Today the children of the community go to the local primary school in Great Gidding, and Robert Van de Weyer, our chaplain, goes weekly into that school to teach the local children.

There are two main differences between ourselves, the Community of Christ the Sower, and the Ferrar household. Our worship is ecumenical; while theirs was Anglican. A number of our members go out to work to earn their own living, full- or part-time, while the Ferrars worked and worshipped entirely in the Giddings.

The pre-Reformation religious orders prayed and worked; the Ferrar family prayed and worked. From the first they had special intercession for the City of London, whence they had come; and prayed that that terrible scourge, the plague, might cease. Today we pray and work. Our day begins with the morning office; one group at 7.30 am, another at 8.30 am (when the children are on their way to school). Together we say Psalms; old and new testament ones. We read old and new testament lessons; we reflect in silence on the Bible passages. We intercede, in a framework of silence, for the world and its needs and for ourselves and our needs; and we give thanks for God's bounty. Our other shared act of worship is the Saturday night Lord's Supper. This is our own ecumenical sacrament; the way we begin the new week together. On Sunday there is no community worship. Each of us goes out to be a loyal member of our own denomination – for part of our ecumenical witness is to remain loyal to our own tradition. The Community of Christ the Sower is not an alternative church doing its own thing; it is a group of ordinary Christian families living ecumenically, but belonging to our own denomination in the area too.

Recently, the chaplain became the non-stipendiary priest in charge of the four local Anglican parishes and two of us became lay elders, whose role is to help the priest in pastoral work. Consequently the involvement of the Community in the life of the locality has grown. Bible study in two parishes developed, in Lent, into study groups in four parishes, with Community members both leading groups and forming a core of these parish groups. Apart from this outgoing ministry into the locality, there are many pilgrims who visit Little Gidding.

Our life here today has grown out of the tradition we have inherited from the Ferrar family. The tradition of hospitality has become a vital part of our ministry. Welcoming groups for afternoons or evenings, for days or weekends; welcoming individuals for weekends, for a week or a month, and sharing our work and prayer with them is a part of our ministry here today.

In the past few months parish groups, both Anglican and ecumenical, have spent a day here. Mothers' Union and Men's Society groups have come for part of a day. Local primary school classes have come for a morning. Individual guests have included young people studying, Friends of the Community, priests having a few days off, Americans interested in the tradition of the place, and Mums wanting a break.

To live here at Little Gidding is to be part of the ongoing work of the countryside. Our five-acre smallholding enables us to produce our own milk and eggs; to grow vegetables and soft fruit; to rear pigs and geese and, occasionally, sheep and beef. To live here at Little Gidding is to be part of the community life of the area – to be involved in the local pantomime or barbecue, the local cricket team or village show. To live here at Little Gidding is to be part of the tradition of prayer and work. To live here is to grow – painfully as well as joyously. It is to experience Our Lord's promise: 'I am come that ye may have life, and may have it abundantly.'

Ann Tilley lived at Little Gidding from 1982 to 1993 when she became a Companion of the Society of Christ the Sower. She has been a non-stipendiary parish worker in the Ely diocese since 1984. She is a member of the East Anglian organizing group for NACCAN (National Association for Christian Communities and Networks), and belongs to the Franciscan Third Order.

Creative Waiting
ELIZABETH TYNDALL

'The lot of man is ceaseless labour, or ceaseless idleness, which is still harder.'

In these lines from *The Rock*, T. S. Eliot underlines one of the major maladies of our time – the division of our lives into work and leisure. This generation seems to have lost the sense of the unity of life with its creative tension of activity and passivity. Our work is our fulfilment, our self-definition, our goal. Without work we lack identity for others and, worse, for ourselves. Time is snatched from an arduous working week; we call this 'leisure' and guard it as a personal good conduct prize.

Unless we have no work! Then our free time becomes not leisure but 'ceaseless idleness', still harder to cope with today than 'ceaseless labour'. Whether it is caused by pregnancy, job loss, sickness, family displacement, bereavement or retirement, the story is so often the same: 'I've become nothing, no one. I've lost my identity.' The work ethic of the last century and the acquisitive society of this have conspired to produce a model of humanity whose life is lived in the separate compartments of work and leisure, with maybe a third labelled 'home'. The walls of these compartments may also serve to provide effective barriers to the inroads of true affection and peace.

Christians do not live outside time and space. We are, inevitably, part of our generation, and some who appear most withdrawn are intimately involved. There are many who lead publicly active lives inspired and upheld only by the silence within. 'We need silence to touch souls', Mother Teresa has insisted to all who work with her as they go about their business of caring for broken bodies. It was strange to imagine her lying in an alien hospital bed, forbidden all her customary activity, and yet so aware of the affectionate concern and prayers of so many. Over eighty, with such a legacy to the world and such an army of followers to administer it, she might well have accepted a few peaceful years of retirement. Could even she have feared the onset of idleness?

Some years ago, John Vanstone wrote a book which has gradually transformed my understanding of idleness. In *The Stature of Waiting* he proposed that the Passion of Jesus was a remembering not so much of the sufferings of our Lord as of his passivity. I am not equipped to deal with the linguistics of this argument but I am still inspired by its potential. For thirty years of his life Jesus lived in relative obscurity – growing, learning, developing and waiting for his time to come. For three years he was exposed to public view. He was active and we believe that in his ceaseless labour he had more effect upon the world than anyone before or since. But this activity, Vanstone points out, was followed by a period of passivity. After his betrayal and arrest Jesus told Peter to put away his sword and from then on he initiated nothing. He was on the receiving end. He was questioned, bullied, cajoled, derided, flogged, and murdered. He did nothing to protect himself, said nothing but to allow 'If you say so'. On the cross his comments were personal and localised. And yet this was the preface to God's great Yes to the world.

'. . . the faith and the hope and the love are all in the waiting.'

(T. S. Eliot 'East Coker', *The Four Quartets*)

If such a time of waiting was useful, or even necessary, for God's purpose at work in Jesus, it is very possible that our times of idleness, apparent uselessness, may be of equal value to our times of productive work and ceaseless activity. We recognise this each time we go on a retreat or withdraw into our private place of prayer. We may fudge the issue by acknowledging that prayer is 'hard work'. But our prayer is also passivity, so perhaps we are on our way to discovering a profound truth. All the same, we may still be far from absorbing this discovery into the reality of our everyday lives.

To be pregnant is to be aware of the new creation which is a part of myself, preparing for the release and separation of another human being. If all goes well, the waiting involved, and the short withdrawal from the world are amply justified. Dare we draw a parallel from this experience to our other enforced times of waiting – when we lose our jobs or our homes, or partners, when we are ill, depressed, when we retire, and even at the end of life when all of these come together to thwart us? Well, perhaps the difference is that we cannot feel the new life that is stirring within us, nor can those around us discern that anything is happening. The waiting can be very painful. We sometimes increase the pain by our own feeling that life is unfair, should not be like this, or through self-flagellation and the fear that we have let someone down.

Life is for living now, where we are, even if it is painful. Ideally, life is for enjoying. Much of the time we fill it with ceaseless labour. But when those times of ceaseless idleness arrive, we might learn to find it easier, instead of harder, if we allow ourselves to enjoy it and to live in the present. This can be done even if there is a lot of pain around. Indeed it is at such times that we catch a glimmering of the truth that pain and joy are two sides of the same coin. In a letter to an elderly ailing friend who had been an outstanding teacher of contemplative prayer, both in and out of the cloister, Archbishop Michael Ramsay put it like this:

> After immense activity one passes into a phase where passivity is the only way. I pray that you may be finding this passivity as the way in which the soul serves God, not by doing this or that but by passively receiving the great streams of his love and compassion.

Elizabeth Tyndall, a retired teacher, is a deacon in the Deanery of the White Horse. She is a Member of the Julian Meetings Advisory Group, conducts retreats and gives spiritual direction.

Dance of Life
ANTHONY VISICK

Before time began
God danced a glorious happy dance.
Father, Son, Holy Spirit
Danced round and round
Singing and laughing with the joy of being.

'Let us making something to dance with us.'

The sun, the moon, the stars
Danced round and round

With the Trinity.
Waves roared, streams sang
Mountains leaped like lambs
There was joy and happiness;
Sun shone through pines
Birds called;
The whole world danced with God.

'Let us make man with free will
Then he can choose to dance with us.'

Man chose not to dance and be happy.
Man chose to go his own way, shuffling
With hate, anger, misery.
No love. No dance. No joy.

'I will become one with them.
I will show how to dance and be happy.
We love men. We make men.
We want men to dance with us.
See, I prepare a banquet for all
Who choose to come.'

Shuffling, joyless, loveless man killed
The Son of God.

'Spirit, go down, raise my Son
To new life, to serve the banquet.
Spirit, stay with men.
Teach them love.
Teach them to dance and be happy
But
Leave them free to choose.'

The Spirit stays.

The Music of Emptiness

YVONNE WALKER

'Music is pleasing not only because of the sound but because of the silence in it; without the alternation of sound and silence there would be no rhythm. If we have no silence, God is not heard in our music.' Thomas Merton

Music is often used as a gentle lead-in to silent prayer, both individual and corporate. When we listen to a piece of music it is the pause or rest in the melody which creates the rhythm in what would otherwise be a continuous wall of solid sound. In the same way a piece of lace without the holes would just be solid fabric. The space or emptiness serves two purposes. It holds things together and keeps things apart. In a busy life, the daily period of contemplation is the silent pause which holds life together, creating the rhythm, punctuating the 'doing' with a pause for 'being'. It also separates us from the preoccupations of 'busyness', providing an opportunity to stand aside and be apart for a moment.

The quiet space and the solitude are not negative non-events, but positive and essential elements in the rhythm of our busy daily lives. Gradually we have to learn in the silence to let God play the melody and create the design in our lives. It involves letting go and letting God take control. It may be a painful experience clearing out the debris and clutter that blocks off God's love, the obstacles filling up the emptiness.

We need to own the space and the emptiness, staying with it rather than rushing to fill it with all kinds of good intentions. We must not be afraid if the space remains empty, for it is precisely in the empty spaces that we learn to centre totally on God; we learn to attend lovingly to the emptiness itself with the faith that this very emptiness is where God is.

Mother Julian was gently encouraged by our Lord: 'Pray inwardly, even if you do not enjoy it. It does good, though you feel nothing, see nothing. Yes, even though you think you are doing nothing. For when you are dry, empty, sick or weak, at such a time is your prayer most pleasing to me though you find little enough to enjoy in it.'

In the emptiness we learn to trust in God – it is particularly hard when we can't understand his melody or when the tune disappears and the pause seems to go on forever. That is when we have to hang on to a love which will never let us go. We come to understand that in music a rest or pause does not stand alone, it only exists if there is a note beside it, however long it may take for that note to be played. In the same way the lace cloth cannot consist of just holes; there have to be stitches round them. What makes the melody and the pattern is the integration of silence with sound and space with fabric. When they become united into a pattern, then they are created into a work of art.

When we interfere and try to control the way that the pattern of our lives should take, there is discord and chaos. It is hard to resist the temptation to do more and experience more; we want to control and achieve instead of letting everything, the fullness and the emptiness, flow together in one glorious rhythm. Letting the unity of emptiness and fullness rest and work, happiness and pain all work together for good and for the glory of God.

It takes courage and not a little soul-searching to put aside the books, the holy thoughts, the clever introductions, and let God lead us into the emptiness where he is and which he fills. But there is one area where we do need to take control, and that is in finding time in our busy lives. This is fundamental for the contemplative in action. If the pauses for silence slip too often and times of quiet get filled in with activity, then the quality of the emptiness soon shows up the difference with more distractions to battle with and difficulty in centring and finding that true stillness.

Finding space is not something to put off for the future. We have to search for it now in our daily routine. It may be as short as drawing a deep breath as we step outside the door into the fresh morning air; it may be as long as a cancelled appointment or that interminable traffic jam. It can be scattered at odd moments through the day, if only we are receptive and perceptive with that inner awareness to see God in all things and to find his pause at any time at all.

Finding that God is more present in the emptiness, letting go our ideas of what the emptiness should be like, and our desires as to how long the pauses in the music should last, accepting God's love and letting it fill the space and overflow into the rest of life, sharing his love with others, *this* is what being a contemplative in action is all about – it is the task of a lifetime!

Yvonne Walker is a member of the Julian Meetings Advisory Group, a retreat leader and public relations manager.

Santiago de Compostela

BETTY WHARTON

> Give me my scallop shell of quiet
> My staff of faith to lean upon,
> My scrip of joy, immortal diet,
> My bottle of salvation;
> My gown of glory, hope's true gage
> And thus I'll make my pilgrimage.

Sir Walter Raleigh wrote these lines when imprisoned in the Tower of London shortly before his execution in 1618. He never went to Santiago, or anywhere else, on pilgrimage. The great shrines of England, honoured by earlier pilgrims, had been destroyed during the Reformation, but Sir Walter, like so many of his contemporaries, knew that life itself is a pilgrimage and visits to holy shrines are an embellishment rather than a necessity.

In earlier times this was not so, and men were sent on pilgrimage as an act of penance, or went believing this to be a sure path to salvation. They trudged or rode for miles, to Jerusalem, Rome, Canterbury, Walsingham and Santiago, as well as to such lesser places as Norwich or Hales. They wore distinctive clothing and were protected by international laws which entitled them to charity and safe conduct. Pilgrims were generally made welcome on the route as they brought business for many, though attacks were made upon the wealthier; in Puenta la Reina on the road to Santiago, a wide river had to be crossed by boat, and the native inhabitants were not above tipping the craft over in midstream and robbing the drowned pilgrims if they thought it worthwhile. So notorious did this become that in the eleventh century Queen Urraca built a beautiful bridge, which is still in use today.

So why go to Santiago, 600 miles from the Pyrennes in the wild north west corner of Spain, from England, France, Italy and Germany? The answer is simple: to visit the shrine of St James, brother of John and son of Zebedee, who was the second recorded Christian martyr, beheaded by Herod with the sword eleven years after the Crucifixion. Tradition states that James had visited Spain during those eleven years and also tells us that James's friends took his body (together with the head) down to Joppa and sailed with it to Spain, arriving in a week! They went right up the Spanish coast to Padron, the nearest harbour to Santiago and buried the body in a stone coffin on a hillside. For about 750 years it was apparently forgotten and no records exist. Then at the beginning of the ninth century, the site of the tomb was revealed by a vision of a star accompanied by celestial music, witnessed by the local bishop, Theodomis. A small church was erected over the site and a monastery founded. The name Santiago de Compostela was born – St James of the field of the star.

All this coincided with the desperate need of Spain at the time. The Moorish invasion was increasingly successful and the Spanish longed for divine help in their struggles. When St James, who had always been the patron saint of Spain, appeared at the head of the army at the battle of Clavijo in the ninth century and defeated Islam, his name was made: Santiago Matamoros – St James the Moorslayer. Not only was he hailed as a sort of St George and Winston Churchill rolled into one, but the miraculous discovery of his tomb made the name of the pilgrimage church famous throughout Christendom.

Pilgrims flocked to St James's shrine from all over Europe: inns, hospices, hospitals, magnificent churches and monasteries sprang up along the route. To the modern pilgrim these present a fascinating historical and religious sequence of experience as one journeys from Bordeaux to Pamplona, Burgos, León and Santiago. From Pamplona one visits Roncesvalles where Charlemagne's paladins Roland and Oliver died, and Charlemagne himself began his pilgrimage to Santiago after his coronation as Emperor in 800 AD. Burgos has a splendid cathedral and the great hospital and hospice of Las Huelgas which catered for wealthier pilgrims. León has another fine cathedral with glorious stained glass depicting the estates of man, and another pilgrim hospice, now a magnificent hotel, of San Marcos.

At the end of the journey, one comes to Santiago and St James. The sarcophagus, indubitably Roman, but now encased in silver, is visible in the crypt under the High Altar. The enormous baroque reredos is covered with carving, all gilded, and above the altar stands a sixteenth-century statue of St James looking benignly down the whole length of the cathedral. Pilgrims climb up behind him and the devout put their arms round him and kiss the cockleshells adorning his cloak. He's just a comfortable size for a good hug!

The cathedral is Romanesque inside and high Baroque outside. The eleventh-century doors, windows, walls and roof are totally enclosed by the later sixteenth-century work which has preserved the former in a most fortunate way. The early West door, the Porch of Glory, is so enclosed and remains one of the finest Gothic doorways in the world. The three giant arches are all carved, with St James in the middle of the central column above the Tree of Jesse with Christ in Majesty above. The four evangelists with their emblems; the four and twenty elders with their musical instruments, encircle the whole. The great prophets are there and the figures smile down upon the crowds beneath. It is an uplifting and enriching experience to pass under the Portico de Gloria and enter the austere nave to view the glorious reredos and St James himself.

At this point it does not seem to matter that the solid historical basis for all this is really rather shaky. On St James' feast day, 25 July, the great square outside the cathedral is packed and all through the year visitors throng the place. Though we no longer trudge on foot but ride in cars and coaches, the pilgrimage can be made just as sincerely as in the eleventh century, but now we hope that we can approach the task more spiritually and with less dependence upon outward manifestations of holiness, for example, relics and indulgences. Staves, scrips, bottles and gowns are no longer necessary and scallop shells are now souvenirs, but Sir Walter's lines stand for all time, as he underlined the true meaning of a pilgrimage.

Betty Wharton, a retired headmistress, is on the Council of Management of the Norfolk Churchs' Trust and a member of the Langham PCC.

Action and Contemplation: A False Antithesis

ROWAN WILLIAMS

Why on earth is the relationship between 'action' and 'contemplation' such a problem for the Christian tradition? Which is 'higher' people have asked, or, how much of one can you get without sacrificing the other? Mary and Martha glare at each other with possessive jealousy, all set to scratch each other's eyes out over the ownership of a soul.

Early monastic thought didn't see the issue in quite that way: here the relation is between *kinds* of contemplation - 'practical' and 'theological'. Not that they defined those terms as we do, ready as we are to assume that theology is inherently unpractical! 'Practical' or 'active' *theoria* (meaning contemplation - or really just plain 'looking') is learning to cope with the fact that our lives are largely reactions to something or other *and* learning that this doesn't necessarily mean that we can't be free. 'Practical' life aims at the sort of condition where we understand rather better the way in which chaotic emotion and unexamined instinct break down our ability to see and respond to what's really in front of our noses. What tends to happen is that we become unhappily aware that our reactions are all over the place, disproportionate and destructive, and then we try desperately to control them or plan things so that we won't be taken by surprise. We get ourselves into patterns of anxiously struggling to dominate situations and people, precisely because we know that we can't trust ourselves in circumstances where we're not in charge. Because this never quite works, we become more panicky and distrustful of ourselves and everything else - and so on, *ad infinitum*.

This, I think, is what the early writers meant by 'passion' - not 'feeling' as such, which we can never be without (and shouldn't try to be), but the way in which we try to impose order on our inner mess by efforts that actually make the mess worse, generating more fear and emptiness. 'Practical contemplation' was seen as the exercise of very prosaic virtues - doing what's there to be done at a particular moment - in such a way that we are gently led away from anxiety and taught to be *present*: precisely what Jesus talks about in the Sermon on the Mount.

This was connected, for the early monks, with the living of a life in which the readiness not always to be looking round eagerly for stimulation and novelty was expressed in a commitment to staying in one place. If you are settled in this way, you *have* to face and cope with boredom and fear without the easy escape route of running away. This means that you have to be present in what you're doing; you have to be *doing* what you're doing, not slipping away into fantasies that have no connection with what you are and where you are - otherwise you will simply go mad, your mental life will cease to have any connection with your bodily reality.

So 'practical' contemplation was a matter of disciplining yourself to be *present*. As and when you learn not always to be taking refuge in inner fugues of fancy, or in anxious and obsessive planning for imaginary futures, you become free to turn outwards in a new way: to attend to people and things for what they are, not for what they can *do* for you, how they fit into your private dramas. This is why the early writers said that the state where you had got rid of 'passion' was the state in which real love, *agape*, was possible. But, of course, all this depended on a single starting point - learning from the love of God in Christ that you didn't have to be miserably anxious and afraid because God had already promised his mercy and welcome to you in all your messiness, and you didn't have to get yourself in perfectly controlled order before God would look at you. And it rested, next, on trying to find a way of life that would somehow express this, steering you away from a desperate concern with being in charge of your situation. The practices of monastic obedience and the dull regularities of daily life in the little cluster of huts in the desert had a lot to do with this attempt to remind people constantly of the real dimensions of Christian freedom.

All very well: what do we do about it, not being fourth-century monks? We can begin, I think, just by learning the simple lesson of how our 'passion' works – of our readiness to avoid the present moment, the present person; to avoid ourselves, our bodies, our concrete circumstances, because they tell us so clearly that we are not monarchs of all we survey. And, while we may not find ourselves in the desert of Nitria, we can make some commitment to disciplines that keep us where we are – in prayer and in our duties and doings overall.

> I used to get a peculiar satisfaction when dressing from pushing my feet into my shoes while pulling up my trousers or pulling my shirt on. *To be doing two things at once*, and thus increasing the speed of the whole tiresome process made me feel that I was saving time with admirable dexterity. Now I try to dress almost in slow motion.
>
> Last night I went down to the kitchen to make myself a sandwich, and back in bed I began to gobble it as I always do, never finishing one mouthful before taking another; and reading, of course, at the same time. *With real difficulty* I put down the book and began to munch with the greatest possible awareness . . .
>
> A multitude of such trivial restraints make up a large part of the work. Boys who gulp their food will *never* get to Heaven.
>
> Philip Toynbee, Part of a Journey

There is more sense and 'edification' in this passage than in a great deal of spiritual writing! It cannot be too much emphasised that this isn't a technique for inner refinement in a vacuum: the plain truth is that we don't learn to love until we've learned to *see*. Hasty, anxious, controlled and controlling living shows how badly we have grasped that we are loved, and how little we are capable of loving, caught as we are in our private dramas. We emerge from this as we begin to *act contemplatively*, doing simple things with what the Buddhists so well call 'mindfulness'. If we can't grow out of our introverted obsessions when we confront material things and fleshly persons, we have little hope of 'contemplating' God ('theological contemplation'). Action and contemplation aren't alternative options or rival concerns. Both are simply to do with how we allow ourselves to be set free from the inability to accept our reality as creatures in a complex world we did not make. We can be set free for the contemplative awareness of the presence and need of others which is essential to any love that is more than self-indulgent emotion; and this is inseparably bound up with our liberation to bear the darkness of God's presence, that reality which is most totally and simply *there*, and which is radically beyond our control and our planning. In a world where we seem increasingly incapable of seeing each other across racial and ideological divides, in which we are more and more the prisoners of terrors and fantasies that we have ourselves generated, nothing could be more important than a discipline of contemplation in its full sense: the ground of action that is not dictated by fear, 'passion', unreality, but by trust and silence before each other as well as before God.

Rowan Williams is Bishop of Monmouth.

Index of Contributors and Subjects

Note that the years mentioned are those in which articles or poems were written or appeared in *The Julian Meetings Magazine* and that the bold numerals refer to the pages on which they appear in this book.